The Apostolic Handbook

SECOND EDITION

COLETTE TOACH

AMI BOOKSHOP

www.ami-bookshop.com

The Apostolic Handbook

Second Edition

ISBN-10: 1626640157
ISBN-13: 978-1-62664-015-3

1st Printing May 2010
2nd Edition March 2016

Published by **Apostolic Movement International, LLC**
E-mail Address: admin@ami-bookshop.com
Web Address: www.ami-bookshop.com

About the Author

Born in Bulawayo, Zimbabwe and raised in South Africa, Colette had a zeal to serve the Lord from a young age. Coming from a long line of Christian leaders and having grown up as a pastor's kid she is no stranger to the realities of ministry. Despite having to endure many hardships such as her parent's divorce, rejection, and poverty, she continues to follow after the Lord passionately. Overcoming these obstacles early in her life has built a foundation of compassion and desire to help others gain victory in their lives.

Since then, the Lord has led Colette, with her husband Craig Toach, to establish *Apostolic Movement International,* a ministry to train and minister to Christian leaders all over the world, where they share all the wisdom that the Lord has given them through each and every time they chose to walk through the refining fire in their personal lives, as well as in ministry.

In addition, Colette is a fantastic cook, an amazing mom to not only her 4 natural children, but to her numerous spiritual children all over the world. Colette is also a renowned author, mentor, trainer and a woman that has great taste in shoes! The scripture to "be all things to all men" definitely applies here, and the Lord keeps adding to that list of things each and every day.

How does she do it all? Page through every book and teaching to experience the life of an apostle firsthand and get the insight into how the call of God can make every aspect of your life an incredible adventure.

Read more at www.colette-toach.com

Connect with Colette Toach on Facebook!
www.facebook.com/ColetteToach

Contents

PART 01

CHAPTER 01

Introduction

Chapter 01 – Allegoric Introduction

The Traveler

With the scroll tucked under his arm, the dusty traveler boarded the heavily laden sailing ship.

A quick look around revealed that he was not the only Traveler on board. There was a group that had paid well for their privilege to be on the ship. Dressed in scarlet and bragging gold trim, there was no denying that they were a class above everyone else.

The Traveler chose not to stand with that group. Their glances down their noses in his direction confirmed his decision. He had seen that type before. Worked with them. Received from them. Left, knowing that he could never be a part of them.

Rambunctious laughter broke his unbidden thoughts of the past and brought them to a brash and burly man leaning and shouting over the edge.

He knew that sort too. Quick to speak. Slow to think. He smiled remembering that he was not very different himself a lifetime ago.

This was not the first journey that traveler had been on and the rest of the passengers seemed like the usual rabble he was used to after all these years of voyage. There were those who were a cut above the rest. Those that thought that they were a cut above the rest.

Then the small insecure man, eyes wide and knuckles white as he grasped onto his luggage. His whole life bundled in there no doubt.

The traveler fiddled with the scroll under his arm. Worn from years of being handled, its edges were torn and faded.

Bound tightly with a cord of leather, it had seen as many voyages as he had. His mind drifting to the many roads he traveled, he wondered if this voyage would be the one to unfurl the mysteries he had studied for so many years.

There was something extraordinary about the scroll. He knew it, well he felt it rather, from the moment it had been placed in his hands.

He had been in a meeting with some friends. It was one of those usual gatherings with others in the neighborhood. Each one was swapping stories and exchanging the usual unimportant conversation. Somewhere in the middle of a heated debate on whether the sheep pen should be rebuilt entirely, or just have another pen added, he was rudely interrupted.

A man that he had not seen before and had not seen since walked into the middle of the group and called him out.

"Come." Said the tall and burly man, looking at him with dark eyes and a narrow stare. "I have a message for you."

Not accepting any response, the man ushered the traveler to a quiet spot and pulled a piece of rolled parchment from his satchel.

Before the Traveler could ask any questions or even have the chance to protest, the scroll was placed with a firm thud into the palm of his hand.

"I have come with a message from The King."

Without giving any time for conversation or argument,

"The road you have been on has now ended. He wants you to know that he has granted your request."

Taking a moment to catch his breath and allowing the traveler a moment to recall his last encounter with The King, the man continued on in firm but hushed tones.

"Do you remember?"

Impatient with the blank stare he got in return. He pressed his question further.

"Do you remember?"

"Ah ...yes, I think. I think I remember."

"You went to the courts of the King and you put in a petition. You petitioned for new land and the opportunity to build a new city."

"Do you remember?"

"Yes ...I remember. But ...how ...I mean, why this way?"

The man snorted. "What did you expect? A parade?"

"No, the King sent me here to tell you, that he has granted your petition, but it will be on his terms.

He will give you the land and he will give you everything you need to build the new city. But first, you must go on a voyage. This scroll will plot your course."

He gave a short moment for the traveler to absorb everything.

The man stared without wavering, waiting until nothing could be heard but the deep rumble of a wagon easing past a group of travelers on the adjacent street.

"Now before you get excited, there is a catch."

Another moment of silence. A pregnant pause to add to the drama of his presentation.

"It is not just any voyage. You must find the right one. The King will send other travelers along your way and they will be there to direct your path. Keep your eyes open because just when you think you are headed in the right direction, it will change again.

So be aware! Watch and listen, because just when you think that you cannot walk anymore, when you think you cannot face another storm, then he will open the way and you will go on your final voyage that will lead you to your destination."

Grabbing the Traveler with a firm grip on either side of his shoulders he gave what was his best attempt at a reassuring gesture.

Then with that, he turned and began to walk. Before the Traveler had the time to reach out and say anything, the man was lost in the crowd.

That encounter had happened quite a few years ago and ever since the Traveler had been on voyage to voyage.

Not every journey was plain sailing and he had on many occasions experienced shipwreck and months lost at sea.

There had been times when he found someone that he was sure would lead him to his destination, but in the end, they either abandoned him or led him in the wrong direction.

He anticipated this next voyage. Would this be the one? After so many years of looking, would this be the one that would explain the pages on the parchment?

Finding a secluded spot on the deck, next to a stack of wooden crates, he untied the scroll and smoothed his hands over its familiar brush strokes.

By Colette Toach

To the unknown eye it looked like a treasure map, but since beginning the journey, he had discovered much more than that. The parchment depicted a journey. A voyage that was in itself the treasure. If he went the right way, if he followed the right clues - he would reach his destination. One he had been born for. One he had desired and burned for his whole life.

Sighing deeply, he reached out to roll it up again when a voice spoke over his shoulder.

"Do you wish to understand the map and the road you have been traveling?"

Turning sharply around, the Traveler was faced with a man a head taller than himself. Well dressed and with a hint of humor in his eyes, he was not sure how to take him.

The words, "Who are you?" were the first to come to him. He had every right to be suspicious after all he had been through.

"Relax" said the fellow Traveler.

"The King sent me. He said that you are ready now."

"Ready?"

"Yes, you are ready, to embark on your most profound adventure and... your *final voyage*.

Your Apostolic Voyage

Your calling to apostolic office is not one that you can make up. It is not your idea to leave everything that you are comfortable with to chase a vision where most folks think you are crazy.

Whether you love it or whether you are afraid of it, the Lord has called you on a journey to rise up as His Apostle. From the moment you received that calling, your life has turned upside down.

You have gone from place to place. Journey to journey. To try and reach that goal. You know it is there. God has promised it to you. In fact, it is like having that scroll tucked neatly into your hand.

You know that you are called, you know that God has given you a direction, but no matter how hard you try, you just seem to fall short on your destination.

Well that is where I come in. Let me introduce myself to you.

I am an Apostle and my name is Colette Toach (hence the name title on the book cover) I understand the journeys that you have been on and the one you are about to embark on now.

If you have just received the call or have been carrying it around with you for some time, the Lord has sent me to you, to help you figure it out.

By Colette Toach

Together we are going to embark on your final voyage. The one that is going to take you into the land that God has promised you.

Together we are going to face the storms, uncover the secrets and bring you to a full conviction of your calling. I will teach you what an apostle is. I will show you what signs in your life identify this calling.

I will explain why you have had to walk the roads you have. I will explain to you what this voyage ahead will look like. Then finally I will explain to you what the land looks like when you get there.

As the book title suggests, this is a Handbook. You will live each phase of your apostolic call with me. By the time you complete the final chapter of this book, I would have led you to a new land where you can step out in confidence.

Confirm your apostolic call. Understand the travails of preparation and training, and then finally, fulfill what God has called you to do. The best part is, you do not have to do it alone any longer. I am here to steer you through the storms.

So come, let us embark on this great adventure. Let us establish your apostolic calling... together.

What an Apostle Is

Chapter 02 – What an Apostle Is

The Transformation

In the last year of my schooling, the boys in our class received what was known as an army call up. At that time, it was compulsory for every male who reached a certain age to serve his country for a few years of national service. It amazed me how young scrawny little boys could leave high school, go to the army and come out of it looking totally different!

Where they were small and insignificant before, they came back taller, stronger and even their characters were different. They may have left school as little boys, but they returned as men. They went through a transformation.

This very transformation is what the apostle will face time and time again during the preparation and training for his calling. The apostle is one who begins as a Private in the army and is made to work his way up the ranks to take his place as a General. He will see his own share of scrubbing and hard work and he will get to revel in the glory of public appearance.

However, there is one thing that the apostle will carry with him always and that is the knowledge that without the agency of the Holy Spirit he is nothing. Without the seal of the Father he is unnamed and without the love of the Lord Jesus he is powerless.

If you can see yourself in this picture then you are well on your way through preparation for the apostolic calling on your life. The road that you have been walking as an apostle in preparation has been a time of letting go and of death. This preparation is for the purpose of bringing you to a point of humility, but also to a place of Holy Spirit power. So join me now as I begin pointing out the characteristics of the apostle practically for you and then on to how you can identify the apostolic calling on your own life.

Spiritual Entrepreneur

1 Corinthians 3:10 According to the grace of God which was given to me, as a wise master builder I have laid the foundation, and another builds on it. But let each one take heed how he builds on it.

The apostle is a spiritual entrepreneur. You can easily identify business entrepreneurship in the world because entrepreneurs are always coming up with these new dazzling ideas. An apostle is the same, but he is a spiritual entrepreneur. He always has new ideas. He is always coming up with a new concept. They may not all work, but it never stops him from trying again. And again. And again. Until he succeeds!

This is probably one lesson we lived the most in the early days of our ministry (Apostolic Movement International). For those who were with us at the very beginning, they will recall the many changes that we went through. We came up with some crazy ideas at times. Some worked, some did not. Each time we tried something new, a pattern began to take shape. Later along the journey, ideas that failed in the past were resurrected with a new element and usually on a grander scale.

There is always something happening on the horizon in the life of an apostle. Just when I was finally reached the goal I would say, "You know what? I was thinking about this new revelation that the Lord has given me. I think we need to go for this idea. I think we need to add something more." Or, even worse..."We are scrapping the whole program and we're starting again! I've got a new direction."

All Things to All Men

1 Corinthians 9:20 And to the Jews I became as a Jew, that I might win Jews; to those who are under the law, as under the law, that I might win those who are under the law;

21 to those who are without law, as without law (not being without law toward God, but under law toward Christ), that I might win those who are without law;

22 to the weak I became as weak, that I might win the weak. I have become all things to all men, that I might by all means save some.

All Ministries

The apostle can do all the tasks in the ministry. He is able to step in and take the place of anybody. If somebody is missing, the apostle is there to fill that space.

The apostle functions in both the internal and the external anointing. He is able to flow with all the gifts of revelation. He can flow from the internal anointing, but when it comes to praying he can also flow in the external, in the signs and wonders and power gifts. (I recommend *The Prophetic Anointing* for more on the internal and external anointing)

All Temperaments

The apostle is also able to function in all the temperaments. You cannot cement him into a specific temperament. One minute he is explosive and expressive, and the next minute he is austere and unemotional. An apostle can be all four of the temperaments or a mixture thereof.

And so if the apostle is an expressive the Lord will take away his emotion. I'm an expressive by nature and I thrive on emotion. Expressives cannot get up in the morning if there is no emotion. We don't feel like it. We can't do anything without emotion. So you will often hear an expressive say,

"But Lord, I don't feel like it."

He says, "Tough, I'm trying to swing you to the opposite temperament. Learn to do without your emotions!"

Or you get the analytical that is totally unemotional and is logical and does things in order. And so, for them, "this is the way things are" and 'this is the way things go'. We have step one, step two, step three. And so the Lord will walk into the life of an analytical and just scramble it to mess with him.

The Lord will say, "Stop relying on your mind. Let's see some emotion there, please," and swing him to the total opposite side.

Then we get the amiable who is a nice guy. He is the nice guy that everybody wants to be around because he is always so helpful and he is always so friendly. He is always trying to make you feel comfortable. But he doesn't like to confront or cause a fuss. When there is a confrontation, he is the guy who will back down.

To this apostle in preparation the Lord will say, "I'm tired of you being so nice all the time. For goodness sakes, get some fire in you and become a driver!"

He will start putting an amiable in confrontation situations where he is forced to confront, where he is forced to change. It is a very painful thing for an amiable when he is used to being so nice all the time.

Or on the other end of the pendulum the Lord will take the driver who usually just pushes his way through every difficult situation. Someone with a driver temperament says, "If I have a brick wall in front of me I'm going to just bash and bash and bash until I get through." No matter who gets in his way, he will push past them to succeed. They make the toughest bosses! They insist on perfection and expect everyone else to have the same drive as them.

To such an apostle in preparation the Lord says, "You need to learn to be nice to people."

He will then put the driver in a situation where, bash as much as he may, nothing is happening. He will be put in a job or be made a pastor, and the Lord will say, "Now you have to be nice to people. You have to listen to their problems and care about them for a change."

So if you have been going through some of these things, it is called apostolic preparation.

All Doctrines

Not only does the apostle have to learn how to change in his character but he has also had experience in various doctrines, denominations and walks of life. He is somebody else who knows everything about everything. He can tell you about the various denominations and walks of life. He has had exposure to the other fivefold ministries as well as the heresies in the Church.

He knows something about everything and if asked a question will always have answers. It will not be because he is more intelligent than most, but simply because he has been made to live more than most! No amount of head knowledge can give you this kind of training. Only by living on the road set up by the Holy Spirit, will the apostle come to this place of completion.

Spiritually Hungry

The apostle is not complacent to just stay in the same place. An apostle never stops growing. He is not complacent to say, "I've arrived. I'm the great apostle. I'm upon my throne and seated, and I have this established ministry."

No! The apostle is too busy jumping ahead to get complacent. There are new territories, there are new horizons. There are new visions and ideas and new goals. There is always something higher and better and greater. And of course with the Holy Spirit, He never runs out of ideas.

The apostle is always growing and moving and expanding. He is never satisfied. It doesn't matter how big he gets, it doesn't matter how much he expands. He wants more. He wants to go deeper. He wants to go further.

The day I stop growing, put me in a box and bury me, because that is the day I die. Because when I stop learning and growing, then I stop living!

By Colette Toach

On the Cutting Edge

The apostle always wants to be on the cutting edge of what God is doing. He is always listening, straining in the Spirit to hear when the next step is, and he is there taking it. When the Lord starts moving the body of Christ he is there before anybody else is. He has heard, he has seen, and usually he is the one who is releasing it.

Strong Leader

He takes responsibility on his own shoulders. You don't have to tell an apostle that he has a job to do. He automatically steps in and takes on the responsibility. If there is something that needs to be done, he does it. If there is something that needs to be organized, he organizes it. When something goes wrong, he is the person who steps forward and says, "I am responsible." So if you are headed for the apostolic and you are waiting around for somebody else to do the job, forget it. You are the 'buck'. It stops right by you.

So a lot of the preparation that you will face as an apostle is learning to be a leader. You will learn soon enough that a Leader not only takes responsibility for his own actions, but also take responsibility for the actions of others.

Trendsetter

The apostle does not wait around for others to tell him what to do, but goes ahead. He doesn't sit around waiting to hear a mighty thundering voice from heaven before he takes a step. He is always in face to face communion with the Lord and he is running ahead of the rest and setting a trend.

As a result, people want to be like the apostle. They cannot help themselves. People look at an apostle and they are drawn to him.

They say, "Now that's what I want to be like!"

They can't help themselves. He is the kind of leader who stands out and motivates others just by who he is.

He not only has the ability to lead but shows others how to lead. Leadership comes naturally to an apostle. He may not have started out that way, but the end picture of what an apostle looks like is that he has the ability to lead. When he stands up and walks, people follow him. He is the kind of person who, if you are standing mulling around in a group, as he steps into the room, everybody notices him.

Air of Authority

The apostle carries an air of authority around him. He doesn't have to say anything, and he doesn't even necessarily have to do anything. As he walks in, you notice him. Not even by the way he looks, but just by the presence of God around him and the authority in which he stands. There is something about him that just draws you. You want to know more about this person. You want to get to where he is and ask a few questions and find out what he has.

He is the kind of person that, if a whole big group goes to a restaurant, the waiter is just somehow drawn to him to make the decisions. Even in the world people will identify the leadership in an apostle, because he carries an air of authority that people want to listen to. When he speaks, things get done! He doesn't have to rant and rave and scream and shout.

When he speaks he speaks with an air of authority that makes people stop and think, "You know what? I should listen to this guy." Did not the soldiers say of Jesus, "never a man spoke as this man?" again and again you will see how Jesus walked with that kind of authority that even the vilest of sinners could identify and be convicted by.

Face to Face Relationship With God

The apostle has had a personal encounter and experience with the Lord Jesus, because it is the Lord Jesus who releases the apostle into the body of Christ. They have had a personal revelation of the Father, the Holy Spirit and Jesus. They know the trinity in His fullness. They know how to function in the fullness of the trinity. They know the holiness and fear of the Father, they know the power of the Spirit, and they also know the love and compassion of the Lord Jesus. They are mature in the fullness in their spiritual knowledge of the Lord.

As a result, the apostle has a solid image of who he is in Christ, and he reflects that image to others. The apostle reflects Christ. When you meet the apostle you know the Lord is with you. You know He is there listening in on that conversation. There is something about him that just draws you, and you know that he is representing Christ. He has that image.

Lays His Own Foundation

The apostle has his own commandment or mandate from God. He cannot call himself an apostle if he is still sitting as a member in the local church. It is not going to happen. It cannot happen, because how could he possibly build a foundation on somebody else's ministry?

Often people want to say of the apostle who is still in the throes of preparation, "Well he's a rebel. He's out of order!"

No. He's just an apostle.

You say, "Well why does he have to leave the church?"

Well where else is he going to build? Where have you seen a bricklayer go into a home and start digging up the floors and saying, "You know what? This house would look better if it had a couple of changes. I'm going to build my house inside this house, and let's see how it comes out."

By Colette Toach

He would be mad. He has to go and get his own piece of land and build his own house and his own foundation.

An apostle has set up an infrastructure for others to follow. The apostle doesn't just give lip service. He doesn't just tell you how to do things. He doesn't just say, "This is right and this is wrong." He actually gives you something to work with. He gives you the tools. He builds the building and he says, "Okay, now this is how you function."

Has His Own Mandate

The apostle has his own mandate and his own pattern, and he may get some of that from various different sources just like the builder gets the mortar and the bricks, sand and everything else from different sources. However, when he puts it together it is his house. It looks like something he designed and he constructed. It doesn't look like anyone else's building. It is unique. The apostles are not going to build the same kinds of houses. They are not all going to look the same. Some of them are going to be brick. Some of them are going to be wood. Some of them will be stone.

Unique Pattern

So you would see a rebel who sticks out like a sore thumb, that does everything different. He has this wayward idea of building something that just looks nothing like anybody else has built. You will know that he is an apostle. You see the entrepreneurial qualities of him always wanting to go out and do things differently with new ideas, new concepts.

They know why they are called, they know where they are called to, and they know how to get there (Well at the beginning they *think* they know how to get there and face a bit of humbling first, that is why they need that phase called Apostolic Training!).

Your Apostolic Calling

Has the Lord told you that He has called you to be an apostle? Have you received an inner conviction of that calling? Then you are well on your way to begin walking this road of apostolic preparation.

Perhaps you have looked at these points I have listed so far and in comparing yourself you might say, "I'm not even close to being an apostle!" If so, then you are right where God wants you to be. For that is what makes the apostle set apart. It is not about you. It is not your ability. It is not your strengths and your great leadership skills. It is about His image. It is what He will take you through and birth in you and make out of you.

You can be nothing right now and you can look at yourself and think, "Oh Lord, I'm too ashamed to even admit that I may have been called to be an apostle." However only when you can come to that place of realization, does the real work begin.

Jesus said to the Pharisees: *John 9:39 And Jesus said, "For judgment I have come into this world, that those*

*who do not see may see, and that those who see may
be made blind."*

*40 Then some of the Pharisees who were with Him
heard these words, and said to Him, "Are we blind
also?"*

*41 Jesus said to them, "If you were blind, you would
have no sin; but now you say, We see. Therefore your
sin remains.*

Because they thought they had arrived and could see,
how blind they truly were! If only they would admit
that they were weak and blind and a failure, because
then the Lord could have done something with them. If
you say to yourself, "I am an apostle, and I have arrived
and I am all I should be." Then how blind you are and
the Lord cannot shape you.

You would be as a hard piece of clay that would
crumble in the hand of the master. What potter would
use such dry and hard clay?

However, if you said to the Lord, "Lord I am weak. I
look nothing like an apostle and I am afraid that I will
fail you," then the Lord can do something with you.
You are clay that is wet and soft. The Lord will then
bring His hand on you to shape and to mold you.

So where do you stand today? Are you blind or do you
see? Are you willing to admit that you need the hand
of the master upon you?

Have you picked up this book out of curiosity? Have you picked it up to try and prove your apostleship? Or have you picked it up to gain God's direction for your life? The choice you make is what will allow the Holy Spirit even now to come upon you and to change you. It is up to you whether you will be a dry and brittle piece of clay or a soft and malleable piece of clay.

If you are soft and weak then the Lord is going to take you and He is going to form you into His image. When He has finished, you will look like this picture that I have painted for you.

Jesus is the one who will do the work. Right now you may just be an unrecognizable lump of clay, but when you are finished you will stand reflecting Jesus Christ in deed and in authority! Can you see the end goal? Can you see the image and the picture? Now God has something to work with and He can take you there!

Identifying Your Apostolic Calling

Chapter 03 – Identifying Your Apostolic Calling

I remember doing a study on the dark ages in a history class once. I was so amazed at how the whole of society came to a sudden halt during that time. Nothing new was invented, the arts died and even the living church slipped into the abyss of obscurity.

Then when the death was at its darkest, a revolution took place in the world! The first printing press was invented and the very first book to be printed on that press was the Bible. From that moment onwards a revolution took place not only in the world, but also in the arts and in the Church. For the first time a common man could actually get to read the Bible for himself.

Just imagine it! Before only a select few held the secrets of the Word of God, but now suddenly everyone could obtain it. It was the beginning of an era where the heart of the Church began beating once again towards God and began to seek the Lord for change and revival. And so the rest, as they say... is history!

Apostolic Revolution

Many centuries later and another resurrection is taking place in the church of Jesus Christ! For as the Word of God was hidden from so many in the dark ages, the truths of the end times apostles have also been hidden from the Church and the world. It has been the mystery of the ages and as the Holy Spirit has lifted the veil from our eyes an apostolic revolution has come to the Church!

Just like before, only a select few had access to the Word and now everyone can have a copy, so also is the Lord making it known that the office of apostleship was not just for the select few of the New Testament, but it is now also available to a whole new generation of believers all over the world. The mystery is indeed being revealed to the Church and it is in progress. Yet the first seeds of this revolution did not begin in the open. It was not splashed all over the newspapers and it in fact took the Church by surprise.

Who would have imagined that in this day and age the Lord would raise up leaders of this caliber? Even more incredible, who would have imagined that the Lord would raise *you* up as His apostle to the Church?

And so while the mystery of the apostolic movement was still hidden from view, the Lord Jesus began revealing Himself to His elect. He began calling them within the bounds of their obscurity and began raising them up while they were hidden from the entire world. Just as in the time when Jesus called His original disciples, so He continues to call unto Himself His apostles so that He might present them as a gift to His church.

Where do You Fit In?

So where does this leave you in the Lord's plan? To begin with, I would like to make it clear that the call to the apostolic ministry does not come in a grand announcement where all of the world can see it.

It comes as it did for a shepherd boy tending his father's sheep. Yes, just like David was anointed in secret, so also are the end times apostles being selected and called out even now in secret.

So the first sign with which you can confirm your calling is to identify when the Lord first called you to be an apostle. It was likely at a time when you were at your lowest and when you least expected it. Yet no matter when the call came, it has become a conviction in you!

First Marker: Personal Conviction

From the day that David was anointed as future king of Israel, he knew what his place was. Do you know what your place is? Do you have a conviction of your calling? If not, then this is the place that you need to begin.

Until you have that inner conviction you will never have what it takes to endure the preparation and training that waits for you. It is not enough to hope or to guess or to rely on the revelations of others. No, you must know in your own heart that God has called you to be an apostle.

This kind of calling does not happen by chance and you cannot make such a calling up. You cannot hope to be an apostle and you cannot try to be an apostle. You are either called or you are not.

David was anointed with oil. There was no doubt in his mind that he was anointed! He experienced the anointing. He saw Samuel hold out the oil to him. It was his experience and no one could take that away from him!

It was this conviction that could take David through the many trials that he would still face from that time and it is the kind of conviction that you also need to take you through. For when you have that conviction, nothing will move you. No amount of rejection will deter you, no amount of failure will phase you and no amount of fire will consume you. You will know what you are and you will know what you are called to be.

So consider this as being the first big marker along your apostolic voyage. Do you have a conviction of who you are? Do you know that God is calling you to be an apostle? Do you know it in your heart without a doubt? If so, then you are ready to begin traveling along this way and you are ready to see what waits.

Second Marker: Confirmation

Along with a personal conviction, you need a confirmation of your calling. Jesus knew He was the son of God from very young. He also knew what he was called to do, but only as He stood in front of John the Baptist the confirmation of His calling came.

Jesus received many confirmations of His calling. In fact, if you follow the Gospels you will see that the Father confirmed who Jesus was to his disciples through personal revelation (such as the case with Peter) and again at the mount of transfiguration.

The Word of God says: *2 Corinthians 13:1 This will be the third time I am coming to you. By the mouth of two or three witnesses every word shall be established.*

It is not enough to just receive the rhema for yourself, there needs to be a confirmation in the mouth of witnesses. This is where the prophetic ministry comes in and the Lord will often use a prophet to confirm this calling to you. Note though that this confirmation will not serve any purpose until you first have your own conviction.

Third Marker: Identifying With the Signs

Then finally as you have received that personal conviction and received the confirmation, you will be able to identify with the signs of apostleship! Now I have already painted some pictures for you on what an apostle looks like, but I want to bring it home now and apply it practically to your apostolic calling.

It is easy enough to look around you and identify the signs in others, but once you can identify the signs in your own life, you will begin to understand a bit about the journey that is ahead of you. The Lord Jesus said that: *Luke 14:28 For which of you, intending to build a tower, does not sit down first and count the cost, whether he has enough to finish it -*

So before you decide whether or not you are going to accept this call and begin implementing the mandate that God has given you, you first need to see if you can identify with the signs of the apostle and then if you are willing to pay the price of that apostleship!

Ten Signs of Apostolic Calling

I will take you briefly through the following ten signs of the apostolic calling. You may be able to identify with all of them, maybe you will not. It all depends on your spiritual maturity.

It might even be possible that the Lord has called you to an apostolic ministry, but you have not faced sufficient preparation yet to be ready for this phase. So if you have received a personal conviction of an apostolic calling, but cannot identify with most of these signs, then give the Holy Spirit some time to work in your life.

In time you will be able to tick each of these signs off as you face the rigors of apostolic preparation.

Sign 1: Set Apart

Romans 1:1 Paul, a bondservant of Jesus Christ, called to be an apostle, separated to the gospel of God.

This sign follows perfectly from what I have shared already. To be set apart means to be appointed. It means to be separated from the rest. If you have received a personal revelation of your apostolic calling, then you are very much set apart!

You can no longer see yourself as a regular churchgoer. Another fire burns in you and you will indeed find yourself separated. You always find yourself on the outskirts of church fellowship and standing outside of the boundaries of "how things are done" in the local church.

You are not complacent or satisfied with how the Church is run and you burn with a greater vision. This discontentment is what sets you apart. If you were content with the way things were and you were accepted by the majority, then you would not be separated would you?

I am afraid that this is a great price for one to be called an apostle and if you find yourself having a need to be accepted or recognized, then you are about to find out that being 'separated' is part and parcel of the apostolic calling.

Sign 2: Spiritual Entrepreneur

> *Galatians 2:6 But from those who seemed to be something - whatever they were, it makes no difference to me; God shows personal favoritism to no man - for those who seemed to be something added nothing to me.*

7 But on the contrary, when they saw that the gospel for the uncircumcised had been committed to me, as the gospel for the circumcised was to Peter

8 (for He who worked effectively in Peter for the apostleship to the circumcised also worked effectively in me toward the Gentiles),

Paul certainly understood this sign of apostleship! He was always different. Even amongst the apostles of his time, he stood apart. Being brought up in the Jewish tradition and trained by the greatest Jewish teachers of his day, the Lord sent Paul to the gentiles! He was indeed a spiritual entrepreneur who did things differently!

He had a vision that the others did not and this is one sign that is prevalent in all who are called to the apostolic ministry. If you are always doing things differently or coming up with new ways to structure the Church, then this is indeed a sign of apostolic ministry.

Your ideas might not always work out, but you are always coming with new concepts and new patterns. You have an idea in your mind at all times of what you would do "if you were in charge" and when given the opportunity you would turn things upside down!

I remember an illustration that an apostle shared with me once. He shared how when he first started out in ministry he was put in charge of the youth group. He was brimming with so many ideas of what he wanted to do. He wanted to implement a complete structure and form a mechanism where each member of the youth would be given a place where their ministries would be identified and then trained in that position.

Of course as he presented his full idea to the pastor, he was faced with a devastating disappointment. The pastor said, "If I had to implement that in the youth, I would have to implement it to the entire church and I am just not prepared to make that kind of change."

This is what makes the apostle stand out! He is not only willing to take chances, but he is also willing to change. Just as Paul was willing to leave his entire Jewish heritage behind and mingle with gentiles, so will you as an apostle be called to change and to rock the boat when everyone has just become comfortable.

Do you desire to bring change? Are you forever changing the "way things are"? Then you can certainly identify with Sign 2 of apostolic calling!

Sign 3: Called by Jesus (Personal Encounter With Jesus. Miraculous Call)

> *Acts 26:15 So I said, 'Who are You, Lord?' And He said, 'I am Jesus, whom you are persecuting.*
>
> *16 But rise and stand on your feet; for I have appeared to you for this purpose, to make you a minister and a witness both of the things which you*

have seen and of the things which I will yet reveal to you.

17 I will deliver you from the Jewish people, as well as from the Gentiles, to whom I now send you,

18 to open their eyes, in order to turn them from darkness to light, and from the power of Satan to God, that they may receive forgiveness of sins and an inheritance among those who are sanctified by faith in Me.'

If you have had a personal encounter with the Lord Jesus and received your calling from Him directly, then you can identify with this sign. There have been many occasions where I have seen the Lord Jesus, but one occasion really stands out to me as the day He called me to be an apostle.

I had been going through a lot of change and I had been struggling with many issues that the Lord had revealed in my life. It seemed to me that the whole world was against me and that I was the greatest failure of them all!

I was standing in my bedroom and cried out to the Lord with all that I had. I cried out, "Lord, what do you want from me?" In that instant I felt as Paul must have when he was struck to the ground. I was brought to the ground by the Holy Spirit as His presence came over me.

In that moment, I was in the throne room of God. I heard the Lord say to me very clearly, "Go heal my people." After a moment more, I heard Him speak again, "Go feed my people." And again, "Go set my people free."

I knew that God had spoken and like Paul I trembled, wondering how I could have been called for this purpose. The Lord Jesus then spoke many other personal things to me during that time and when He had finished, I felt Him place His hand upon my shoulder and tell me to stand. I stood up knowing that God had called me.

I stood up knowing that I was called to be an apostle and I stood up knowing my purpose and place in the Kingdom of God. It is that calling that has remained as gold through the many fires I have faced since and it will remain my foundation until I have completed every mandate that God has given me. Then I will pass that foundation on to the next generation.

If Paul had not received that miraculous call on the way to Damascus, he would not ever have known who he was. Before that time, he really thought that He was doing the work of the Lord. Before that he felt that he was being the best Jew that he could be.

How misdirected he was! He was correct in knowing that he was called, but not until his conversation did he know his place and purpose.

So you too need such a call before your apostolic training can begin. This call might in fact usher you directly into apostolic training. This goes way beyond an inner conviction. This is a miraculous and personal call directly from the Lord Jesus. Such a personal encounter will change your life and such a calling will set you firmly toward the goal of apostolic office.

Sign 4: Early Call (Called From Womb)

Galatians 1:15 But when it pleased God, who separated me from my mother's womb and called me through His grace,

When exactly does the Lord call the apostle? Is it when he makes a commitment? Is it when he decides it is a good idea? Well in Paul's case, he was called from the womb. At first glance this seems like a strange comment. If you take a look at Paul's life, you will note that for the first part of it, he persecuted the Christians! He was very far from being an instrument in the Lord's hand.

Yet even in his sin, Paul hungered for God. Even as he persecuted the Christians, he did it in zeal for the Lord. If you can identify a hunger for the things of God from a young age, then this too is just one sign of an apostolic calling. You might not have had a full knowledge of God or understood what was happening, but even in your heart as a child, you hungered for God and sought after him.

You might have been brought up in a Christian home and known the Lord all of your life. Either way, the apostle is one that is born with an awareness of God and searches after God with all that is in him.

Sign 5: Trained in Secret

> *Galatians 1:17 Nor did I go up to Jerusalem to those who were apostles before me; but I went to Arabia, and returned again to Damascus.*
>
> *18 Then after three years I went up to Jerusalem to see Peter, and remained with him fifteen days.*

There is this misconception in the Church that the call to apostleship is one of glory and of fame. As you continue with me along this journey you will come to discover that the complete opposite, is in fact true!

If you take a look once again at the life of Paul, you will notice that the first thing that happened after he was called is that he spent 3 years in Arabia in obscurity to be trained. Paul was not the only one who was trained in secret. You hear nothing of Jesus until He was already trained and ready to implement His mandate.

David was sent to the wilderness, and poor Moses to the backside of the desert. Thousands of years later the same principles are still being applied by the Holy Spirit and so as one called to the apostolic ministry you will find the foundation of your calling in obscurity.

Now this can be particularly hard for someone who has a desperate need for recognition, but until you have been trained in secret, you will not be ready to rise up in the public eye.

So if you were active in ministry or in your church when you received your calling to the apostolic ministry and then everything fell apart, then you are right on track. If you suddenly find your ministry opportunities drying up and everything being taken from you, then take heart! If you have literally been dragged by the Lord from the pulpit to the backdoor of your church, then rejoice, for it is just another sign that confirms your apostolic calling!

Sign 6: Rejection and Opposition

> *1 Corinthians 4:10 We are fools for Christ's sake, but you are wise in Christ! We are weak, but you are strong! You are distinguished, but we are dishonored!*
>
> *11 To the present hour we both hunger and thirst, and we are poorly clothed, and beaten, and homeless.*
>
> *12 And we labor, working with our own hands. Being reviled, we bless; being persecuted, we endure;*
>
> *13 being defamed, we entreat. We have been made as the filth of the world, the offscouring of all things until now.*

This picture that Paul paints for us is certainly not a pretty one! Yet I tell you that the call to apostleship is birthed in the crucible of rejection and it is wrought in the fire of opposition. Have you ever tried lifting weights to tone up your muscles?

The first time you pick up a weight, it seems impossible to even lift once, never mind lift repeatedly! However, as you pit your muscles against that weight time and time again, your muscles grow in strength until you can lift a greater weight.

Now you might look at someone who is lifting weights and say, "Why on earth would you do that to yourself? Why go through all that pain?" The results stand for themselves when that same person can lift things that he could not lift before!

Rejection and opposition are the spiritual weights that strengthen the apostle. As he pits his conviction and spiritual strength against all that comes his way, he finds himself standing to overcome storm after storm. Facing and overcoming the rejection and opposition is what will make you fit for the Master's use.

I remember the first time that I was openly opposed in ministry. I was so devastated! I was told that I did not speak for God and that I was in deception. I felt like a wannabe weight lifter lifting a heavy weight for the first time. It was heavier than I expected! As time went on though, I overcame each phase of opposition and I grew stronger until such accusations did not move me any longer.

Looking back, I thank the Lord for these times because they have enabled me to overcome many storms along my apostolic walk. So if you are facing rejection and opposition from your family, church and friends

By Colette Toach

because of your calling and all your "new ideas" then rejoice!

Not only is it a confirmation of your apostolic calling but it is a tool in the hand of God to forge you into the apostle that He has called you to be.

Sign 7: Called to Forsake Everything

> *Philippians 3:8 Yet indeed I also count all things loss for the excellence of the knowledge of Christ Jesus my Lord, for whom I have suffered the loss of all things, and count them as rubbish, that I may gain Christ.*

Here is a point that every apostle will relate to.

It is not good enough to be prepared to die for Christ. You must be prepared to live for Him!

There are many who would proudly confess that they are willing to be a martyr as Stephen was for the Lord, yet when the same kind of person is asked of the Lord to give up their bitterness, their materials, possessions or even a relationship, suddenly the price is too high!

You will find that the call to apostleship will cost you more than just your life. It will cost you your family, friends, material possessions and even your country. Paul knew this well and the greatest price for him was to let go of his achievements and great learning.

Watchman Nee shares and example in his book, *The Normal Christian Life,* of a man who truly desired more of God. He dedicated his life to God but there still lacked that "something". When he went to the Lord in prayer, he said to the Lord, "Lord I desire more of you and I am prepared to pay any price for it." The answer he received was not what he had expected.

You see this man had only one passion in life. That passion was to complete his doctorate and to wear the title "Dr." in front of his name. He gave everything else up to the Lord and even went into ministry full time, but this is one thing he desired more than anything.

So you can imagine how he must have felt when the Lord said to him, "The one thing I require of you is your doctorate. I ask that you give it up for me." This was a painful decision for this man to make. He begged and pleaded with God.

He said that he would pay any other price than this, but the Lord's decision remained. So just two days before he was to hand in his qualifying examination that would give him the title he had worked so many years for, He wrote his examiners and told them that he would not be completing his studies after all.

Now to you it might seem that the Lord was being harsh with this man. Why couldn't the Lord just let him have the doctorate? Well that man could have had his doctorate and sacrificed the anointing for it, but he came to realize that this doctorate was something that he could boast in and not something the Lord could boast in.

By Colette Toach

Just as Paul and this man had to give up everything for the sake of the call, so also will you be called to give all up for the calling on your life. It will never be said that you rose up because of your great abilities or your great learning.

Rather it will be said of you that you are an example of the grace of God! Your boast will always be in the Lord and this is why you will be called time and time again to lay all upon the altar for the sake of the call.

At times you might not have understood this and thought the Lord unfair. Perhaps you were tricked out of privileges or lost honor that you really deserved. If so then rejoice, for it is another sign that God has called you as an apostle and that His hand has been on you to prepare you.

Sign 8: Suffering for the Call

2 Corinthians 1:6 Now if we are afflicted, it is for your consolation and salvation, which is effective for enduring the same sufferings which we also suffer. Or if we are comforted, it is for your consolation and salvation.

7 And our hope for you is steadfast, because we know that as you are partakers of the sufferings, so also you will partake of the consolation.

It is difficult to understand why suffering must come for the calling on your life when those around you are affected. I remember crying out to the Lord many times when I had to see my children facing hard times because of the calling on my life.

I went to my father and aired my frustrations and my anguish. He just smiled and said to me, "I faced the same thing when you were a child. I also cried out to God. But I have come to know that if it had not been for those hard times you had to face, that you would never have grown up into what you have become in the Lord."

This caused me to rethink my life and also realize that the suffering that the apostle is called to face as part of his preparation is both a privilege and a necessity for their mandate. With each conflict I have faced and overcome, it has given me the weapons and knowledge I need to help others overcome.

Paul said it so well in the above passage. He said: *"because we know that as you are partakers of the sufferings, so also you will partake of the consolation."*

Because of the suffering that Paul had to endure those under him were consoled, because he faced the sufferings for them. Just as Jesus went to the cross and faced death for us, so also will you be called time and time again to face sufferings and to overcome them for the sake of others.

The Lord has chosen you as His vessel and to be effective you need to have the life-changing answers that will revolutionize the Church.

By Colette Toach

That kind of wisdom and those kinds of answers can only come to you in one way...through sufferings. So if you have faced more hard times than the average believer and you seem to experience one wave of difficulty after the next, then rejoice! For this is another sign that you are called to the apostolic ministry and it is also the tool of the Lord to prepare you to be effective in ministry!

Sign 9: Call to Leadership

> *Romans 11:13 For I speak to you Gentiles;*
> *inasmuch as I am an apostle to the Gentiles, I*
> *magnify my ministry,*

Paul was never satisfied to be a follower. He thought as a leader and acted as a leader and as a result the Lord could use him. There are many sheep but few shepherds, and so with the call to apostleship comes a call to leadership. This sign lines up with the others in that to be a leader you are set apart and you also face much opposition and rejection. You will do things differently and will not be afraid to do so.

What is a leader? Firstly, a leader is someone who has followers! Do you find people are drawn to you without you having to do anything? Are you the kind of person that people look to for answers? This denotes the beginning of leadership.

A true leader is one that takes responsibility for his actions and the actions of others. Paul was such a leader and never forgot his failures and successes. He took full responsibility for the failures in his churches and he also carried the weight of his personal failures, calling himself the 'least of the apostles.'

The Lord could use Paul because he was willing to follow the Lord instead of man. Are you the kind of person that has never been content with following? Perhaps you are always asking questions and looking for the truth for yourself. Then this is another sign of your apostolic calling.

The apostle seeks to know the truth for himself. He does not just accept anything everyone says, but listens and then seeks his own revelation and conviction. He is discontent with the meager bits of teaching and truth that are handed out and seeks more. Then as he receives that abundance from the Lord, he hands it out to those around him.

The leadership qualities in the apostle in preparation might not be easy to see from the outside at first. But if you take a look within, you will see a divine discontentment with the way things are going and a spiritual restlessness with the mediocrity of the Church.

Such a discontentment and restlessness denote an apostolic ministry and if you can identify with that then be encouraged for you are not in rebellion; you are simply called to the apostolic ministry!

Sign 10: Has a Pattern – The Old to the New

1 Corinthians 3:10 According to the grace of God which was given to me, as a wise master builder I have laid the foundation, and another builds on it. But let each one take heed how he builds on it.

Just like the prophet has the ability to see the spiritual hunger in the people of God, the apostle has the ability to see the flaws in the old church structure, desiring to usher it into the new.

The apostle is as a master builder who will look at a structure and notice all its weak points. If you find yourself going to church services and noticing its cracks and flaws, then this too is a strong apostolic orientation.

If something is your trade, you find that you cannot even mingle socially without it affecting you in some way. Using again the illustration of the builder, if building is his trade, he cannot go into a single building without noticing it. He will be inspecting it to see if it matches the correct standards and what would improve it. Now does this make the builder rebellious or out of order? Not at all, it is just who he is, he cannot help himself.

The apostle is the same. He does not try to be out of order, but he simply sees things in the church system that others do not. He sees the things that are correct and the things that are incorrect and cannot help himself but to judge every church or ministry he comes across by those standards.

You are always wanting to let the people of God know that there is a "Promised Land" where things are different! You desire to show them a better way and a new building that does not have the flaws of the old.

Now if you have this orientation, it is not to say that your judgments are always correct. You may begin with an apostolic orientation, but your early judgments are likely to be based on your own ideas and preconceived notions.

This is why apostolic preparation and training is necessary, to ensure that when you do rise up into apostolic office that you judge according to the Lord's standards and not your own.

In Conclusion

If you could identify with these points, then it is clear that the Lord has called you to an apostolic ministry. Like I said earlier though, you cannot even begin this journey until you have received a personal conviction and confirmation of this calling.

The call to the apostolic ministry is not a simple matter of having a ministry of prophecy or compassion; it is a call to the highest ministry office and as a result comes with the greatest price.

The price that you will be called to pay will not be one of monetary value. Who could have prepared Abraham for the sacrifice of Isaac? Was he not prepared to offer God all he owned and all that he had? Yet the Lord required of him the thing that was dearest to him.

So as one called to the apostolic ministry you will also be called to give up anything that stands in the way of your calling. If you dedicate yourself to this calling and accept what is being offered to you, then know that the price of your pride, of your zeal, of your emotion of your strengths and weaknesses will be required of you.

The fires of apostolic preparation will strip you of everything you are and the molding of apostolic training will change you into a new image. Into the image of Jesus Christ.

CHAPTER 04

Set Apart

Chapter 04 – Set Apart

How many mischievous things did you do when you were a child? This was the subject that came up one evening as Craig and I began to swap stories of our childhood. I came to the conclusion, as I listened in disbelief, that little boys misbehaved a lot more than girls did!

Craig shared how he and his childhood friend used to get up to mischief when they could escape the watchful eyes of their mothers.

One story in particular that appealed to me was when they discovered a treasure of military gear that his friend's father had kept from his army days. The boys were having the time of their lives.

They put on the helmets and uniform and as Craig described it, I could imagine two little boys running around pretending to be soldiers in their oversized gear. Then they discovered a harness amongst all the gear and decided to take their world of make believe up a notch.

Excitedly they strapped the harness to a tree and then each one of them took turns to tie themselves to the harness and launch themselves from the branches, pretending to parachute. All was going well until a mutual friend came along and asked if he could join.

Things did not go as they had hoped though and instead of swooping down with the grace of a bird, their friend fell wrong and landed right on his head! They soon came to realize that this gear that they were playing with was not a toy and that perhaps they did not know what they were doing.

They had the picture in their minds of what they wanted to do and they had the uniform. They were brimming with ideas and ready to take on the world, but their plans did not always turn out the way they wanted.

Each time they came up with new ideas, there was always a catch and someone would end up with bruises, scrapes or burns. But this did not stop them and they continued to come up with more and more things to do.

They may have felt and looked like soldiers, but they had a few things to learn yet. Well, both those little boys are grown up now and they have stopped flying out of trees or playing with gasoline, but they have also learned a few things about life. They have learned how to get an idea and make it work without serious injury and they have learned how to plan properly with hindsight.

Looking Ahead

The apostle in preparation is very much like these little boys. The apostle is always brimming with ideas and new concepts, but at the beginning, things do not always turn out the way he planned.

Instead of reaching the goal he had anticipated, he ends up rejected, falling on his head and usually wandering in the desert for a few years. Yet this never stops the apostle from coming up with new ideas time and time again. He is an entrepreneur and it is what sets him apart in the Church of God.

The apostle is not like other believers who are content to remain on one spiritual level. When others are rejoicing over a wonderful Sunday service, he is at the drawing board trying to figure out a way to make it go better. When church leaders and members are busy working hard at raising funds for their new church building, he is hard at work, putting together the blueprint for the end times church.

The apostle is never content with the way things were and he is far from happy with the way things are. He thrives on taking the Church of God beyond their complacency and he revels in setting each member in their place and seeing that blue print put into action.

However, before any of this can become a reality, such an apostle in preparation comes to learn a thing or two. He comes to learn that what he sometimes thinks is a great idea, is more than likely a "flesh idea."

And so he is brought to place his many concepts and blueprints upon the flame of the altar time and time again. It is only when he comes to the place of spiritual readiness to let go of everything he is and everything he is capable of, that the Holy Spirit can begin training him for leadership.

Against the Grain

If there is another element that makes an apostle stand out, it is that he hungers after something new and wants to stand out. We live in a society where no one wants to stand out. If you look or act differently to other people then you are considered strange or a rebel.

Yet who do people follow? People follow those that are different and who are not afraid to be different. People follow the trendsetters of the world and they will even sacrifice their own individuality to be conformed to their image.

Everyone would like to think that they are unique, but at the end of the day, you will find a group of sheep simply following after the sheep in front of them. However unless there is a Shepherd, who will lead the sheep?

Then again, who is willing to look different and be that shepherd? Everyone wants the acclaim and there are many who desire to be apostles, but do not realize that the greatest price they will have to pay is that they will never be normal.

I remember my own frustration as I grew up. Being a Christian, I did not fit in with any of my peers in the world. But being a pastor's daughter, I did not fit in with any of my Christian peers either!

I was always left dangling somewhere between earth and heaven. For years I tried to fit in and to force myself to adjust. But then I would say or do something that would make it clear that I was different.

I always seemed to go against the grain and I never wanted to do the same thing twice. I came to learn that people did not want "different" and that they liked "change" even less! Yet as an apostle these two words will always be with you.

If this has been your life story, then welcome apostle in preparation! You are in for the ride of your life! Jesus was not normal and neither will you be. Jesus was always upsetting people. He embraced sinners and scorned the "righteous."

He chose a motley crew for His disciples and was not afraid to speak out and teach things that were unheard of before. It was these very qualities that made Him a leader. It was His boldness that caused people to follow after Him and it was His uniqueness that caused them to remain.

You need both boldness and a unique mandate to complete the work that God has for you. However, before you can even begin applying that mandate, there needs to come a change in you.

By Colette Toach

Firstly, you are going to need to address all your insecurities. You cannot be a leader that has a fear of man. Sure enough, you could try to act like a leader and pretend to be something you are not, but until you have the kind of godly boldness that Peter had, no one is going to get healed by your shadow.

Next you will need to stop being a follower and become a trendsetter. You might always have had the ideas in your mind, but maybe you never stepped out to try them. You need a balance.

You need both confidence and boldness to step out and be different. You are called to be a trendsetter and the time will come when the Lord will want to place others in your care. Unless you have dealt with your weaknesses you will fail. Unless you are willing to try and fail, you will fail in the end also. So where does this leave you?

It leaves you up on the cross as the Holy Spirit begins forming you to the image of Christ. It is in His image that you will become a true apostle. If you think that you will stand up and be acknowledged for the great leader that you are, then you have already lost sight of what you have been called for.

You are being called to represent Christ to the Church. You are to be His hands and His feet extended. Only then will you begin making the changes that the Lord desires to do in His Body.

The Secret Chamber

The road called apostolic preparation is what will bring you to a place of readiness to accept this pattern. It is the road that will lead you to the secret chamber of Christ where you will learn who He is and what burns in His heart. It is in this chamber that you will put your head to His chest and with each heartbeat hear His plan for you and for His church. Then you will go out from that place and implement His pattern.

It begins with Jesus and it ends with Jesus. With each time you lay your head upon His chest, you will be conformed to His image until you resemble Him and think like Him and act like Him.

Then as you reach that place, you will reflect His glory and all the patterns, visions and desires that were planted in your heart over the years will be put into place and you will be able to see the greatness of what He has for you and where He is leading you.

You have been chosen by His hand to do a task that few are being called to do. You are called to take the Church upon the crest of His glory and to usher them into the promised land that awaits them. This will not come without a price.

And so as you pay the price of being set apart and standing afar from others; as you pay the price of never being normal and as you pay the price of failure, death and sacrifice, you will look within and begin to see the gold that glistens.

By Colette Toach

But press on, because this is just a foretaste of what is to come. Sooner than you know, that small sparkle will break out into a radiant glow of glory until you are so covered by it that when others look at you they will see the face of Jesus Christ!

May that be your prayer and may that be your desire, for as you decrease, He will increase within you. That is what being an apostle is all about and it is in that glory that you will find your mandate.

Birthing Your Apostolic Ministry

Chapter 05 – Birthing Your Apostolic Ministry

After giving birth to my first two daughters, I was looking forward to the experience for the third time. I prepared for the birth of Rebekah Jade Toach (Ruby) with the same zeal I did with the other two, expecting it to be similar.

In fact, I was more optimistic this time because I had just participated in one of our international conferences and had been in the spirit for a whole week prior to her birth. I was on cloud nine and felt ready to birth this baby into the glory!

I counted the days until the time came and sure enough two days after the conference the big day finally arrived when I began to experience those familiar contractions. I eagerly packed my bag and headed for the clinic with Craig.

This was going to be quick and easy. After all, the more babies you have the easier it gets right? Well that day I discovered that birthing a baby was not always the same and that each child is unique. Hours into the labor, my contractions began to slow down. So I was induced. Strong contractions came again. But just an hour later, they had slowed down again.

So I was given a stronger dose of medication. This went on for a while until after being in labor for the whole day the doctor decided on an epidural to help get the baby out.

I was adamant though that this baby was going to be born in the glory and we spent the whole time pushing through in prayer. Craig prayed each contraction through with me and by the time I was wheeled into the operating theatre, the spiritual world was more real to me than everyone else around me.

However even in that, the complications persisted. This baby had decided that she just did not want to be born. I huffed and puffed and pushed and travailed and with each wave of contractions, the doctor, myself and Craig were urging this baby to come out!

I was fast reaching a place of exhaustion and when I felt that I could not possibly huff or puff one more breath or even raise myself to push any longer, Ruby suddenly thrust forward and was born. With the sound of her piercing scream in the room, I laid back. Exhausted, Relieved and pleased that the ordeal was over.

The Birth

The birth of your apostolic calling is much like the birth I just described. It seems that you are pregnant forever and then when you feel that the Lord is finally releasing you to begin functioning in your calling, you find yourself being held back time and time again.

So you try again with great zeal and try to push through. But again you face another death or another disappointment. Does this mean that you are not pregnant? Does it mean that your baby will not be born? Not at all, it means that you just have to press on a little more!

Changing Shape

A baby is not conceived and born in a moment and neither will your ministry. There needs to come a time of maturity and growth before you will be ready. Trying to have the baby too soon will result in its death. Very often when the Lord calls someone to the apostolic ministry they feel that they have to get out and begin acting like an apostle. It is no surprise that they end up with so many disappointments.

When a woman conceives a child, you do not even see the proof of that child for some months. There has to be a time of growth and maturity. A change needs to come in yourself and as a woman's body changes to adapt to her child, so also will your life begin to change as the Lord begins preparing you for the calling on your life.

You will need to make a few adjustments for this ministry baby. You will need to let some things go, like your temperamental traits and strengths. You will need to overcome a few things, like your weaknesses and fears.

By Colette Toach

From the day that you receive the conception of the apostolic child in your womb, you will begin to face change. You will begin to go through a metamorphosis and at first you will be the only one who notices anything.

When I was running to the bathroom with morning sickness, I was the only one that was aware of the baby in my belly and the havoc it was wreaking with my body! So also those around you will not be able to identify with the changes and hard times you will face in preparation for this calling.

There will be times when you will have to face the trials alone and just like Craig could be there to hold my hand through this whole process, I had to face each change and pain alone. I had to embrace it and overcome it.

In the same way, as you learn to face each issue that the Holy Spirit brings up in you and as you learn to submit to His change in your life, you will be very aware of the new life that turns inside of you. The apostolic calling that has been conceived in you must be real to you before it is real to anyone else.

It is you that will birth it. It is you that must walk it out in fear and trembling and it is you that must embrace it. No one can do any of those things for you. No matter how many people tell you that you have an apostolic ministry, until you have the conviction for yourself, you are not even at the starting point yet.

This is why at first you will find yourself alone and having to face tough times that try your patience and the very mettle of what you are. It will shake you to your core and change the very root of who you are.

Then, only once you have embraced this calling and have submitted to its work in your life, will others begin to see the change in you.

It was an exciting time when I began "showing" that I was pregnant. I no longer just looked fat and soon everyone could tell that I was having a baby. It seemed in those next five months that I changed overnight and everyone rejoiced with me.

So do not get discouraged if the Lord has called you to be an apostle and no one has acknowledged you yet. Press on and allow the Holy Spirit to keep changing you. It is during this time of change that you will suddenly be noticed by those around you.

You will no longer have to tell people, "I am pregnant with an apostolic ministry" because it will be obvious. The way you walk, the way you stand and the way you talk will reflect that calling. Nothing you do in yourself however can bring this change! I could have tried wearing maternity clothing or stuffing a pillow down my shirt to look pregnant, but only time and change made my belly stand out.

So if you are trying to convince others that you are called, then stop right there. Forget about what everyone thinks and begin working on yourself. Until

By Colette Toach

you change within, they will not see the change without.

Until you die to what you want, they will not see your resurrection and until you allow the Holy Spirit to lead you to places that you might not want to go, others will not notice the change in your walk.

Changing Your Mind

I firmly believe that the reason the Lord made humans to carry babies for longer than most animals is so that it would give us time to adjust! It is no secret that humans do not like change and certainly something like a new baby in the house changes things.

Sure we all have these fairytale ideas of what it would be like to have the pitter patter of little feet in the home, but no one prepares you for the sleepless nights and the chaos that ensues.

I am sure that you have a picture in your mind of what kind of an apostle you will make. If you cannot see this yet, then you have a picture in your mind of what another apostle looks like. It looks great! You can see the authority and the power and the leadership ability. You have likely built up so many pictures that are based on your own desires and what you have seen in the Church.

But nothing can prepare you for apostleship until you have been there for yourself. So let me take your hand and help you along the way by bursting your bubble a bit. If you think that you are facing death and a struggle now, it is nothing compared to the death and pressure you will face standing in apostolic office.

There is no such thing as suddenly "arriving" in apostolic office where the deaths stop and the fun begins. Not at all, the birth of your apostolic ministry will just be the beginning of a long and arduous journey.

So the Lord will take you through preparation first to gear you for what lies ahead. It is during this time that you will learn how to die to the flesh and what an apostle really is. He will change your wrong mindsets and begin showing the vision he has for you within your heart.

If you look at the disciples as an example you will see that their real work only began after Peter gave the first gospel message. When they walked with Jesus they only received a taste of what was to come.

In fact, they had it pretty easy while Jesus was still around. Jesus carried the load for them and He was there to fix things up when they failed. But when Jesus ascended and they received the baptism of the Holy Spirit, only then could they begin.

From that moment onwards you will notice the hardships that they had to face. They had not been jailed or beaten before that. But as they began fulfilling the mandate that Jesus had given them, they began to pay the price for that calling.

However, when that time did come, they were ready for it, because they had spent three whole years with Jesus getting ready for the calling on their lives. So you will also find yourself going through many different stages of change and travail to prepare you for the ministry God has called you to.

But let it be very clear in your mind from the beginning that it will not be what you had anticipated and if you cannot handle what the Holy Spirit is giving you now, then you will not be able to cope with the intensive training or standing in apostolic office later.

Moses and David had it just as tough! David endured three years in the desert before he was appointed king of Judah and Moses was eighty years old when he was sent to set the Israelites free of their captivity.

These things do not happen overnight and the one thing you need to keep in mind is that this preparation is not for God's sake, but that it is for your sake. The Lord would use you immediately if you were ready right away, but that is never the case.

Once again, it depends on you how long your preparation will take. David learned to change quickly, Moses took much longer. Maybe Moses was more stubborn. Who knows! I do know that until you are ready God cannot use you.

If you have the same fear of speaking like Moses did, then you will have to overcome that first. If you have a need for others to accept you and recognize you, then you will be chased to the desert like David was.

It all lies in your hands. The Lord will use a willing and ready vessel; it is up to you how soon you will be ready. But perhaps you feel a bit like I did on that operating table. You have tried and you have pushed, but still you do not see the fruits of your labor.

Perhaps you are struggling to identify what God wants you to do. Maybe you are facing so many different conflicts in your life that you cannot make sense of any of it. If this is where you are, then you need a doctor to help you get this baby out and you need someone by your side to encourage you.

Enduring Travail

I was told time and time again while I was pregnant, "You have nothing to worry about. Women have been giving birth for centuries now. It is a perfectly natural process!"

Well if that was the case then I could have propped my head up with a pillow in bed and pushed that baby out over a nice cup of hot tea and my favorite cookies. But the reality of it is, not everything goes the way that it 'should' go.

There are many apostles who have been called who insist that they can do this thing on their own.

"God has been raising apostles for centuries now; he can surely raise me up!"

Well then you are better than Peter and Paul because both of them needed some help to rise up into apostolic office. But we will look at them in greater detail along with Moses and David in a later chapter.

Yes, God has been rising up apostles for centuries, but He has been raising them up through the agency of man and if you would like to press past the travail and on to holding your baby, then you will need assistance to help you along this journey.

Faithful Support

Even with the doctor helping me birth the baby, I could not have faced each contraction without my husband Craig who was faithful to the end. He was there to hold my hand when the pain was intense; he was there to encourage me when I felt that I would give up.

If there is one thing that you will need throughout this journey, it will be the closeness of knowing Jesus in an intimate way. It is one thing to know the glory and to operate in the anointing, but when the anointing has waned and you are left alone with your flesh being exposed, there is only one who will understand what you are going through.

There will be times along your journey when you will feel totally isolated. You will find yourself standing in a crowd, feeling completely alone. You will look around you and not understand anyone else. Even worse, others will look at you and not understand what you are saying.

With each contraction, there will be times when you will feel like giving in. It is at times like this that you will need your loving Savior to coax you through the rocky waters, for only He can understand the humiliation. He also knows what it is like to be nailed to a cross half naked. He also knows what it is to be scorned and beaten. And with each time that you are forced to face these hard times, it is Jesus who will be there to console you.

A Lonely Walk

The apostolic walk can be a very lonely one at times and if you do not have the Rock to fall upon you will not have the strength to continue. In my own experience, there have been times when I have felt that no one in the world understood or cared. Even though I knew that this was not true, in my heart I felt alone and abandoned.

In those times, it was in the quiet of my room and in the sadness of my tears that Jesus stepped in and carried me. In fact, it was during these times that I made the quickest progress. When I had learned to lean on Him and forget the pain of travail that I was in, I looked up to see that I was further ahead than I realized.

By Colette Toach

So if you find yourself in travail right now and you are struggling to keep your head above water, then your only recourse is to run to the rock, which is Jesus Christ. He will hold your hand and He will understand when no one else will.

He will give you the strength when all you can see is your weakness and He will encourage you when all you have succeeded in is failing. Jesus will have an answer every time to every need and every struggle that you will face.

Do you want to begin building a solid foundation for your apostolic calling? Then here is where you need to begin:

> *1 Corinthians 3:11 For no other foundation can anyone lay than that which is laid, which is Jesus Christ.*

Jesus will be your foundation. He will make sure that your ship stays afloat in the harshest storms and He will help steer you through the jagged rocks. When you and your ministry are built upon the rock, Jesus Christ, you will be able to handle any storm. You will have the strength to face every contraction and you will have the ability to endure any amount of pain to birth the apostolic ministry within your spirit.

Being Conformed to the Image of Christ

Chapter 06 – Being Conformed to the Image of Christ

Making Gold out of Sand

Have you ever tried your hand at making pottery? I got the opportunity to take some pottery classes once and it was the most fun that I ever had. It was quite exciting to take a lump of dark clay and then shape it until it began resembling something.

Then to varnish it and put it in the fire. The best part though was to take it out the oven and see the colors of the varnish come out and what was just a lump of clay was now a beautiful ornament!

I heard a story once of how a lady had even made a full dining room set for a party. She made the plates, cups and saucers to match. Then after the party was over, she no longer had use for all those plates and had a new project in her mind of what she wanted to do with the clay.

So one by one she smashed the plates and ground the hard clay down again, wet it and reused it. You see the plates no longer served their purpose and before she could reuse that clay, it had to be ground up nice and fine and then reshaped.

This story lines up with a very simple and short dream that I had one evening.

I dreamed that I was a clay pot and as I stood there, I saw how that pot was smashed. I awoke knowing very clearly what that meant.

It meant that the vessel I was, was about to be smashed. It meant that the Lord had completed His work for the vessel I was and needed to conform me into a new image.

Remember the scripture I shared earlier: *2 Timothy 2:20 But in a great house there are not only vessels of gold and silver, but also of wood and clay, some for honor and some for dishonor.*

Well I had been a vessel of earth and now the Lord was smashing that vessel to make a new one. As I went to ask the Lord the fullness of what it meant, He gave me this song:

I Smashed the Old
By: Colette Toach

I smashed the old
I take these shards in My hand
I am forming something new.
Raising you out of the dust
Making a vessel of Glory.

Chorus

When you begin to see my
Nail prints in your hands.
When you walk and see my
Nail prints in your feet.

When you stand and see my
Piercing in your side.
Then you will know,
Yes you will know,
That you are being conformed
To my image.

Then you will stand
Rivers pouring from your mouth
With a new heart in your breast.
For the heartbeat will be mine
You are my vessel of Glory.

You see, you are that piece of clay just like Paul speaks about in:

> *"Romans 9:20 But indeed, O man, who are you to reply against God? Will the thing formed say to him who formed it, "Why have you made me like this?"*
>
> *21 Does not the potter have power over the clay, from the same lump to make one vessel for honor and another for dishonor?"*

To be transformed from a vessel of dishonor to a vessel of honor, it will take being smashed into shards. It will take being ground up into sand and so as your life and ministry are taken and ground into the dust; you are taken on a life-changing course to make you into a glorious vessel of honor.

By Colette Toach

And so from the moment of having that dream, a transformation took place in my life. Everything that worked before did not work any longer! What I did before did not fit any longer.

I felt like a baker trying to cook with the tools of a mechanic! It seemed that one day my job description was, 'mechanic' and then suddenly I was thrust into a kitchen and made to be a baker!

Have you ever had that happen in your life? Where you were walking along your spiritual road and you were coping just fine and then suddenly the same principles just did not work anymore? Where before when you gave counsel to a specific type of person, it worked, but when you tried the exact same counsel to the exact kind of person again, it did not work?

Perhaps you were used to getting into the presence of the Lord in a certain way before and now when you try the same things, He just seems to have moved premises? If this is happening to you then do not despair. In fact, it is good news! It means that the old is being smashed to make way for the new.

The portion of faith you had before, is not good enough for this new vessel. The portion of anointing that you had before barely scrapes the bottom of this new vessel and the love you had before is not sufficient to carry this new vessel.

And so there comes a transformation in your life. There is nothing comfortable about having that initial pot smashed and for a season you may feel like a ship being tossed to and fro! Yet the Lord is doing something very miraculous in your life! He is taking the clay vessel you were and He is transforming you into a vessel of gold.

He is taking the shepherd boy and making you into a king! He is taking the renegade youth and making him the leader of a whole nation. He is taking the servant and making him into a master and he is taking a child and making him into a successful ruler.

None of this came easy to the models that have gone before you and it will not come easy to you either. But press on through and when the fires of preparation burn out the dross that is in you, keep your eyes on the vessel of gold that lies ahead. God is indeed making gold out of sand!

Why Can't God Make Up His mind?

It is during trials like these that you will find yourself asking this question, "Why can't God make up His mind?" You were sure that He told you to go in a specific direction and to pursue a specific calling and then suddenly everything around you begins to change.

From functioning as a youth pastor, he changes your course and tells you to start evangelizing the lost. Then just when you get used to that, He tells you to stop going to church all together! What is He doing?

With every single direction that you take, the Lord is building something new into you. I have had the opportunity to train the Lord's Apostles and when I first meet a perspective student I have to smile at the very similar stories they share.

I will always ask on a first meeting, "What burns in you for ministry and what do you believe the Lord is calling you to do?" I will often get a response where the person will share what burns in their heart for ministry and then also what the Lord had called them to so far.

They will share prophetic words from their past and journals from years ago where the Lord told them to pursue a specific call or a specific kind of ministry.

Years later they are still trying to fulfill that destiny, not realizing that the Lord called that word to death a long time ago because it had already served its purpose. The word expired! It was used, over and done. It was no longer needed.

This is something you need to realize along your journey. The Lord will lead you in many directions to bring about character changes in you. It does not mean that because the Lord gave you a word that you should minister to children that you have a children's ministry and you should stay there.

It is very likely that the Lord took you into that realm of operation to train you and to change the vessel you were. Once that job in you is complete, there is no need for you to carry on there.

Do you understand now why you were moved around so much? Do you understand now that you did not miss the Lord?

Yes, it was the Lord's will for you to pursue that word and direction, but it was also His will to let it go once it had accomplished in you what was needed. Many times you will not even feel like you accomplished anything and will walk away from that time feeling like a failure. But be encouraged. The Lord knew exactly what He was doing and in time you will come to use those skills and experiences in your mandate!

Sand From the Foundations of the Earth

> *Ephesians 1:4 just as He chose us in Him before the foundation of the world, that we should be holy and without blame before Him in love,*

From the day the foundations of the earth were laid you were called to take your place in the body of Christ. But sometimes it takes you a while to figure that purpose out! Sometimes you get so busy with your own agendas that you do not hear the voice of the Lord to find out where you are meant to fit.

Yet to become something of worth in the Kingdom of God, you need to begin at grass roots. You need to allow the hand of God to come upon you and make you into sand.

So what is the characteristic of sand? Sand is tossed to and fro with the wind. It cannot settle long in one place. It can be easily picked up and thrown. It is not at all solid and sturdy.

Are you the kind of person that needs to be in control of your destiny? Have you got everything all nicely figured out? Do you have your mandate laid out all neatly and you know exactly what you are doing? Then this could be the main reason that the Lord is taking you on this journey.

You must never forget that your destiny is in His hands and that your control is in His plan and not your own. The minute that you set things in stone and dictate what you will do and where you will go, you become a misshapen piece of hard clay that is of no use to God.

And so as always, before the Lord can lift you up in the eyes of man and use you as a mighty vessel, you will be called to lay everything you have and everything you are upon the altar to be consumed by the fire. Right now you do not know what God has planned for you in the long run.

Do you dare to dream? Then begin by laying aside the dreams you have now. Only when you let the present die, will your future resurrect with a new foundation and an expanded ministry!

CHAPTER 07

Apostolic Preparation and Your Models

Chapter 07 – Apostolic Preparation and Your Models

Standing in the Storm

I could never understand why as a child we were always moving. I was almost embarrassed to let people know that I had been to 12 different schools in my lifetime and had lived in more cities than I could remember.

My first journey began at the tender age of five where we left the country of my birth, Rhodesia, now known as Zimbabwe, in Africa. My parents moved to South Africa and I have faint recollections of the plane ride over and how exciting everything was.

That was just the first move of many though and once we had moved to South Africa, I saw myself being shifted and shunted from one town to the next. As a child I could not understand why things were the way they were, but I learned quickly how to pack and get used to a new school, make new friends and even learn new languages.

I could never get complacent and only now can I see in hindsight how the Lord had been preparing me for the apostolic function.

When I finally left home I rejoiced that the days of traveling were over for me! I was looking forward to setting up my little home and going on my merry way. I had these crazy notions of being a normal mother, with a normal home, normal kids and a normal husband.

One would think that after the many years of preparation that I would have gotten the point by then! But like I said before, "normal" is not a description of an apostle and just when I thought that Craig and I would settle after having our first child, the Lord had us on the move again.

Circumstances caused us to move in with parents, move towns, change jobs and have more kids than we anticipated. Then in the midst of this flux, the Lord called us to leave our country and fly two days to a destination where we did not know what to expect.

Everything changed. It changed daily and where I only had to change friends and schools before; I was faced with changing cultures. Not only was I moving cities this time, but I was going to a country where English was not even the first language. Only those years of being moved around could have prepared me for this big leap of faith.

Stand in the Storm: The Vision

After we had been living in Mexico for a few years, the Lord gave me a vision. I saw a great tornado approaching me as I stood in an open field. Then it picked me up and I was drawn right into the middle of it.

My feet left the ground and the next thing I knew, I was being carried by this great wind. There was thunder and lightning in this wind and I knew that I had just stepped into the middle of a raging storm.

As I was carried, the sound of thunder deafened me and my hair was being tossed by the gusts of wind to such a degree that I could not even see where I was. I tried to struggle with the wind, but it was useless because it was stronger than I was. Then in the vision the Lord told me to let the storm carry me and to stop struggling.

So I let myself go and just let the winds carry me. I felt myself being carried over many lands and often not knowing if I was the right way up or upside down. I submitted to the buffeting and let my body go limp.

Then as suddenly as I was picked up, I found my feet touching the ground again as the storm dropped me on solid ground. Standing tall, I looked up to see that the storm had cleared entirely and that I was on a new land with the sun shining on my face.

Only in the months to come would I fully understand this vision and the implications of it. In this very picture you will get a glimpse of what the apostolic calling is all about. Because only when you are in the storm can you be carried and lifted from one level to the next in your calling.

Perhaps you have found yourself in such a storm throughout your life. Have you asked the Lord, "Why?"

By Colette Toach

if so, then you are right where He wants you to be. I cannot tell you the amount of times I said to the Lord, 'Why me Lord?"

I must have looked and sounded very sorry for myself a lot of the time and I can imagine the Lord almost sighing and thinking to Himself, "Let me give this girl a helping hand here, because she is just not getting it!"

It took me a long time to figure out why I had to face all the changes that I did and that is why I am here to help you out of a few years of trying to get the revelation for yourself. As an apostle in preparation, the ground on which you stand will never be solid.

You will continually find yourself being carried from one situation to the next. There will be times where you will not know which side is up and which is upside down, but if you can submit to that storm, you will find your feet on solid ground soon enough.

When you are suspended somewhere between heaven and earth however, you may feel that you will never reach solid ground. It could be that you have changed jobs, friends, family and maybe even houses so many times in your life that you do not know what is going on.

You look around you and everyone seems to have a track to run on, but each time you try to get on a track of your own, it is disrupted and you find yourself starting over again; and over again, and over again.

Perhaps you are holding on to one small hope in your heart. A hope that says, "If only I can get through this, then everything will begin to settle and I can get moving." Well I have some bad news for you.

Things are never going to settle and you are already moving. You are just moving in a direction that you did not anticipate. Just as I could not see where I was going while in the storm, so will you question, cry out and even argue with God along this journey.

But rest assured, because while you cannot see where you are going, God knows exactly what He is doing and has His own road mapped out before you.

Moving on to the New

I believe that the main reason that the Lord often hides the direction of our roads to us is so that we do not mess up His plans. It is so easy for you to become too comfortable and to begin adding your own ideas to His plan. That is why you are never allowed to become complacent. The apostle is called to take the people of God out of the old and into the new!

So you will continually be pressing on towards the new. Then when the "new" has become old, you will be moving on again. It will feel sometimes that you are always a couple of steps ahead of the rest of the Body of Christ and rightly so, for the leader is set ahead of the sheep to show them the way. The minute you settle and refuse the hand of God to change, you will step back and become a sheep that will be reliant on following another shepherd.

Living the Lesson

The call to apostleship is not one of glory as I am sure you are beginning to realize. If there is a ditch in the road, then you will be the first to discover it to lead the others around it. If there is a hidden thorn bush in the road, you will be the first to step on it, likely barefooted, so that you can make sure others do not walk into the same mistake.

So the storm and the living that you will face as an apostle would seem to revolve around the many mistakes and failures that you have made. If this has been the case, then welcome to apostolic preparation for you have indeed been a willing vessel.

No one told you that there was a catch to being an apostle, did they? Did you think that being an apostle was standing in an exalted spiritual state and being admired by many? Well how did you think that you would rise up to such a position? By being good enough?

No. The Lord needed a willing vessel to go ahead of His people and to clear the way before them. So as you learn through bitter experiences, you will be able to teach God's people effectively how *not* to do it and also the right way of doing it.

Preparation Versus Training

So in a nutshell, apostolic preparation is learning how *not* to do everything. Apostolic Training is learning how to *do* everything right. Is it no wonder that preparation can take anything up to 40 years and training just 3?

There is a lot of learning ahead of you apostle, and most of it will be in the crucible of experience. There is no escaping the fires of life that will shape and change you according to the pattern that God has for your life.

So if your life has been full of hard times and difficult experiences, then be encouraged. While you were in that storm, you were being prepared for the apostolic calling.

Taking Ground

Looking at the experiences that I described at the beginning of this chapter, I could not see very clearly when the Lord was changing my life so drastically. I could not understand why I had to move so much. I could not understand why I had to keep making new friends and adapting to different kinds of people.

In my understanding I was a failure and could not get anything right.

As I stood in adulthood, I saw the journey that I had traveled and saw the many lands that I had passed over. I saw the giant leaps I had made in my personal life and in experience. I learned what *not* to do in many different situations. And I learned how to lean on the Lord and place my head closely to His chest.

So even though you might not see the change or the progress in your spiritual walk so far, be encouraged, because the time will come when your life will be plotted out before you and you will identify the markers along the way and the progress you made.

When a marathon runner is running the race, his weariness often blinds him to the ground he has covered. At times one patch of road looks like the next and it does not feel as if he is getting anywhere.

But if that runner presses on and endures, he will look up suddenly to see the finish line just ahead of him. So do not get discouraged when your failures outweigh your successes and do not give up when you think that you have stepped backwards instead of forwards. Everyone who has ever been called of God has been there!

Examples From the Word: Your Models

While you are facing the storms and marathons of your life it often feels as if you are the only one in the world who is facing these trials! Rest assured that since the beginning of time, there were others who suffered and endured the same. According to scripture they were set in place for our models.

So let's take a quick look at some of our models and the storms that they had to face in preparation for their calling.

Jesus

When the Holy Spirit appeared to Mary and made her pregnant with Jesus, I doubt that she expected to face the hardship that she did. She began by traveling to her cousin Elizabeth. Jesus was barely conceived and already he was on his first journey.

The next journey Mary made was when she was heavily pregnant. Off she was to Bethlehem and then Jesus was barely two when Joseph was warned in a dream to flee to Egypt from the wrath of Herod.

They were not allowed to become settled there either and Joseph received another word to leave Egypt and go to Nazareth. Again and again we see Jesus being moved and his life being changed. At twelve they went up to Jerusalem and then the day came when he was revealed to the people as a light coming from Galilee, where he began his ministry.

If you follow Jesus throughout His ministry, you can barely keep track of the changes! He called disciples, and then sent out 70. Then another time most of them left Him when He shared how they were to drink his blood and eat his flesh.

He never stood still for a moment! He was always doing something new and heading towards a new destination. So much so in fact that John tells us that all the books in the world could not have contained all that Jesus did in those three short years!

If you want an example of what to expect in apostleship, then take a look at the life of Jesus. If from birth he was carried into the storm of change, do you think that you will escape the gusts of wind and the thunder in your own life?

Be prepared for change and learn to get used to it, because the life of an apostle is not a stagnant one.

David

David is also a good example. From the day that he was anointed by Samuel everything began changing in his life. He was taken to the courts of Saul as a psalmist and Saul's armor bearer.

When war broke out, he was back with his father's sheep. Then he entered the scene again and slayed Goliath. Back in Saul's court he married Michael and befriended Jonathan.

David was not allowed to become comfortable. He found himself fleeing from Saul and running to Samuel. From there he ran to the cave of Adullam and on to Gath and Ziglag.

In a few short years, David was fast becoming familiar with various parts of the land. One would have thought that once he became king that things would have changed.

But alas it was only the beginning. He was always on the move. If he was not bringing back the ark, he was fleeing from Absalom or seeking the Lord to retract that hand of the angel of destruction at the threshing floor of Araunah. (2 Sam 24:18)

David never had a time to rest and right up until the day he died, he was overcoming the plots to take the throne of Israel from Solomon.

There is no time for rest and complacency for the apostle, from the day you are called and until the day you die. Change and rearrange will be as common to you as the changing of clothes and the eating of food.

Moses

Moses knew this storm also: *Exodus 20:18 Now all the people witnessed the thunderings, the lightning flashes, the sound of the trumpet, and the mountain smoking; and when the people saw it, they trembled and stood afar off.*

Moses' storm began as early as birth from the time he was placed into that basket upon the Nile until the time he returned from the wilderness. The storm remained in his life as he journeyed with the children of Israel.

By Colette Toach

Then as Moses looked upon the storm upon the mountain top, he ascended into it and it was here that he saw the glory of God!

Embracing the Storm

I have had those who have come to me and asked, "how can I pass through this preparation quicker? Is it possible?"

Yes it is possible, but it will cost you the price of your will. Because the only way that you will make progress is by embracing and submitting to the storms in your life.

As you identify the hand of the Lord in them, you will allow them to carry you to the place that God wants you to be.

You need to come to the place where you will say,

> *"Habbakuk 3:17 Though the fig tree may not blossom, nor fruit be on the vines; though the labor of the olive may fail, and the fields yield no food; though the flock may be cut off from the fold, and there be no herd in the stalls -*
>
> *18 Yet I will rejoice in the Lord, I will joy in the God of my salvation.*
>
> *19 The Lord God is my strength; He will make my feet like deer's feet, and He will make me walk on my high hills."*

For when you can come to that place of trust in God and in knowing that He is indeed in control of your life, then He will set your feet as hind's feet and will make you to walk upon your high place! You need to remember always that you are not responsible for making yourself into an apostle, but that it is up to God to change and shape you.

It is up to you to submit to that change and to allow Him to carry you to places that you do not want to go. You are not able to take yourself to where God wants you to be. Do not think that God needs your help.

All He requires of you is your faith in His ability and your heart of love toward Him. Do you trust the Lord Jesus enough to carry you where you need to go? And again, do you love the Lord Jesus enough to know that He will never cause you to face a temptation that is above what you can bear? Are you willing to hold on to the hope of your salvation with every breath that is in you?

The secret to passing through apostolic preparation speedily lies in having faith in God, knowing the love of Jesus and resting in the hope of the promises He has given you. This is a journey where you cannot make up the rules as you go and it is not a journey that you are in control of.

Just as a leaf is carried by the wind and has no power to direct where it wants to go, so also are you being carried by the wind of the Holy Spirit even now.

By Colette Toach

Submit to His will and allow yourself to be carried. Die to your ever present flesh that insists on 'knowing' and 'understanding' and 'controlling'. Hand over your 'need to know' to the Lord and trust that He can see where He is going. Let go of the need to understand what is going on with you by resting in the knowledge of His love.

When you know His love for you, then you do not need to be afraid of where He will take you, because you will know that He would never harm you. Then let go of your need to control by keeping your eyes fixed on the promises that He has given you.

You will make the greatest progress along this journey if you do nothing but ride the currents of the storm that has come upon you. The greatest sacrifice will be your flesh and the greatest reward will by the authority of Jesus Christ as you rise up to stand as His apostle in this End Times Church!

Death of a Vision

Chapter 08 – Death of a Vision

In the first months of coming over from South Africa to go into fulltime ministry, Craig and I faced a stark reality. The reality was, that ministry was not all about glory and fame.

We had packed just a few months before with dreams in our hearts and minds of what might be waiting for us.

We had built up pictures and hopes of what we wanted to do and what burned in us. We were full of zeal, we were full of ambition... we were full of flesh. The ideals we had in mind differed from what the Lord had planned and instead of the outbreak of revival that we were expecting, the Lord led us to the basement of apostolic preparation!

Have you ever heard this statement, "The elevator to the penthouse begins in the basement?" Well we learned exactly what that statement meant. The first task that I was given as a team member of this international ministry was to handle all the correspondence and to take care of the cooking!

Craig was given the exalted position of gardener and for a long time if I ever needed him, I could be sure I would find him up to his elbows in grass and weeds.

However, in the midst of carrying out these seemingly menial tasks, the Lord had begun a work in us that we would only see years later.

By Colette Toach

Right there with dirt under his fingernails Craig was learning to become all things to all men. It reminded me of David who sat taking care of his father's sheep as his brothers got all of the glory.

At times it sure felt that we were taking care of sheep and there were days when I felt more like an overworked mother than the apostle that God had called me to be.

David

Craig and I would often look at our circumstances in confusion saying to ourselves, "So this is what it is like to be in ministry?

But just as David, who became the greatest King that ever lived, we learned to watch sheep. We learned to be servants. I learned to answer correspondence after correspondence, spending hours in counseling and taking care of people's problems.

Craig would spend hours taking care of our problems and seeing to it that the rest of the team could function in the ministry without having to worry about the day to day care of the home. After all, someone has to watch the sheep.

Often we feel that the best person for that job is the person who is least capable of ministry, but I tell you that until you have learned to watch the sheep and do those menial things, you are not ready to become the apostle that the Lord has called you to be.

You might have the passion, the dreams and the desires, but without the living experience and the ability to relate to anyone on any level, you will not make a very good leader at all.

Well as we began putting out teaching, Craig had come to a place in his spiritual life where he felt that if he was ever going to put out a teaching that he had learned in the year since we arrived, that it would be called "The Way of Gardening!"

It was at this very point that the Lord took him out of that and thrust him into becoming an active part of the ministry team. He rose up fully into prophetic office and seemingly overnight was an essential part of the team. From there the Lord lifted him up even further as an apostle and leader of an international ministry.

Again I am reminded of David who within days found himself from being an outlaw in the wilderness to being placed as king over Judah. Imagine the dreams David must have had from the day that Samuel anointed him. He was called to be king, and yet it would seem that everything went against him from that day!

He was made to care for the sheep and when he finally did make it to the courts of Saul, found himself in trouble yet again and was forced to leave and run for his life. Death after death David struggled with the desires of his heart and the many disappointments he faced along the way.

However it was only when David had learned a few things and had become a leader, was he was ready to be a king. He had to go through a bit of training first.

I can imagine that the last thing David was thinking about, while camping in the land of the Philistines, was being appointed as the king of Israel. It seemed impossible and I wonder to myself how many times he thought that maybe Samuel missed it or was wrong.

But within just a few short years from the time he ran from Saul, David found himself upon the throne of Judah and then on to being king over all of Israel.

Peter

As Jesus walked the earth, the disciples each had an idea in their minds of what their ministries would be. They saw themselves remaining as Jesus disciples and becoming known throughout the land. In fact they all debated over who would sit at his right hand in heaven.

They saw themselves being with Jesus forever. But the Lord had a different idea of how this would come to pass.

When Jesus asked of His disciples once, *John 6:67 Then Jesus said to the twelve, "Do you also want to go away?"*

Peter replied to Him,

John 6:68 But Simon Peter answered Him, "Lord, to whom shall we go? You have the words of eternal life.

They could not see themselves functioning without Jesus. They had dreams and so many goals.

Then the unimaginable happened. Jesus was taken captive and crucified. They were devastated and were scattered. What were they to do now? Everything they had imagined and dreamed about for the last three years fell around their feet in three short days.

Peter tried to hang on as much as he could and followed Jesus into the courtyard, but there denied Him. He ran from that place bitterly disappointed and as he wept he died to the visions he had of ministry. He gave it all up.

I could imagine Peter saying to himself, "I might as well just go back to fishing! This whole idea was stupid to begin with." In fact this is exactly what he did and in this passage we see Jesus calling Peter who had taken his boat out to fish.

John 21:3 Simon Peter said to them, "I am going fishing." They said to him, "We are going with you also." They went out and immediately got into the boat, and that night they caught nothing.

4 But when the morning had now come, Jesus stood on the shore; yet the disciples did not know that it was Jesus.

It was when Peter had finally come to this place of letting everything go that God moved. Only now was he ready to receive the vision that God had for him. Up until this point Peter had all these grand ideas of what he was called to be, but until he let those ideas go, God could do nothing with him.

While Peter still thought that Jesus was going to be the Messiah who would overthrow the Roman government, he was blind to the Savior that was sent to overthrow the Kingdom of Darkness!

When Peter forgot about his dreams and visions, the Lord stepped in and replaced his death with a glorious resurrection and fresh vision. Now Peter was ready to receive his mandate.

> *John 21:15 So when they had eaten breakfast, Jesus said to Simon Peter, "Simon, son of Jonah, do you love Me more than these?" He said to Him, "Yes, Lord; You know that I love You." He said to him, "Feed My lambs."*

Are you seeking God for direction? Are you asking Him for your mandate? The reason that He is not speaking yet is because you are holding on to the old one. Until you let go of the old, your mind will not be able to comprehend the new. You cannot have both. One has to go and for your sake I pray that you sacrifice upon the altar everything that is in the past.

Only when you are willing to let go of what you think you are called to do and also what you want to do, will you be ready to receive the mandate that the Lord Jesus has for you.

Sure enough, when Peter walked with Jesus on the earth, the Lord gave him many promises! He promised Peter that he would be the rock for the Church. He gave Peter the keys of the kingdom. But until Peter let all of that go, he could not begin implementing any of those promises.

Why? Because Peter only had half the picture! He had no idea what Jesus was going to accomplish on Calvary and he had no idea the power the resurrection would hold.

Many of the parables that Jesus spoke were so misunderstood by them. Time and time again they would have to ask Jesus for clarity. Only after Jesus resurrected did they 'get it'

> *Luke 24:6 He is not here, but is risen! Remember how He spoke to you when He was still in Galilee,*
>
> *7 saying, 'The Son of Man must be delivered into the hands of sinful men, and be crucified, and the third day rise again.'"*
>
> *8 And they remembered His words,*

Only when they saw the picture in its finality could they begin to implement it. Peter was always bumbling into things trying to make the vision come to pass and each time he failed. He rebuked Jesus for speaking of being crucified and he cut off the soldier's ear when Jesus was captured. Nothing he did worked!

Only when Jesus resurrected and gave him the full picture could he see in hindsight where everything fell into place. Just like Peter you might have an idea in your mind what you want to do in ministry and where you want to go, but until you receive that full picture, you are not going anywhere!

It would be like receiving only half a painting and deciding what the other half should look like. The problem with that is you will add things to the painting that should not be there. You are making an uneducated assumption. You are doing the same thing in your apostolic calling, if you are chasing after a vision that you think is complete.

Give that vision to the Lord now and put it on the altar. I can promise you that if you will allow the Holy Spirit to consume it, that He will carry you on His wings and take you to a new level.

But if you insist on holding on to your old revelations and bygone promises, then you will only remain in the wilderness longer.

Moses

In fact, you will remain there as Moses did until every last shred of your vision has died. Moses also grew up with a vision in his heart.

He knew that he was called of God to deliver the Israelites and the book of Hebrews tells us that, *Hebrews 11:24 By faith Moses, when he became of age, refused to be called the son of Pharaoh's daughter,*

But just like Peter, he only had half of the picture. He had no idea what God really had in mind. How could he have imagined that God was going to part the Red Sea for them? In his human understanding, could he have imagined that God was going to rain bread from Heaven and cause water to come from a rock?

No, his human mind was limited to the things that he could see and as a result he took it into his own hands.

Just like Peter, he failed! He killed the Egyptian and in the end had to run for his life! David, Peter and Moses all had to run for their lives, because they all came to learn that when God gives you a mandate that He will give you what you need to accomplish it, His way.

God does not need your help to put this picture together and He does not need your natural strength. All He needs is your availability.

Moses spent forty years in the wilderness before God called on him again. By the time he saw that burning bush, thoughts of the Israelites were far from him and he no longer saw himself as the great deliverer.

And so it was at this exact point of weakness and of being stripped of everything, when he was ready! Only when he was nothing, did God begin to unfold the glory that awaited.

So learn from Moses. Because if you hold on to your own ideas of how you are going to implement the vision that God has given you, then you will never know what really waits.

You are trying to do with your human arm something that only God can do. You can try and strive towards your goal, failing all the way. Or you could let that vision die and then stand back and watch as God opens up the sea before you and drowns your enemies behind you.

It is up to you. You are at the place right now where you must choose.
Do you desire to see the impossible? Then let go of everything that you think you know and sacrifice what you want to do. Because I have a little secret for you, "You do not know what God wants to do!"

Just like Moses could not have anticipated the ten plagues of Egypt, so you will also stand in awe as God steps in where you left off. Be prepared to be amazed, but first be prepared to die.

So how long will it take you to die? It took Moses 40 years. It took Peter just a couple of days. It is up to you. If you are weary of dust being in your eyes, then perhaps it is time for you to let go of your vision.

If you have no vision left, then rejoice for now the Lord can begin leading you to the Promised Land! Only when you reach your destination will you see how everything falls into place and how, without your knowledge, the Holy Spirit was plotting a course for you that is exactly on beam with every plan and pattern He has for you!

Time to Give Up

So begin now by writing down every vision that you had for ministry. Be sure not to leave out any points. Make it as detailed as you can. List the entire vision, structure and the lay out. List where you see everyone fitting into that vision and what part you see yourself playing in it.

Then once you have written it all out, not leaving out a single thing, take that piece of paper and burn it. Yes, you heard me correctly. Burn it.

I cannot take you to the next step in this journey until the old has been laid upon the altar to be consumed in death.

You see, it is only when you come to that place of submission and willingness to be anything, that the Lord can use you. Only when you are willing to lay aside your dreams, desires and ambitions can the Lord begin setting you in place.

You may be called to the apostolic ministry, but right now there are so many veils of flesh that are covering your view that you cannot see the mandate that God has for you.

Your eyes are colored with your own ideas and your own patterns. You are like the little shepherd boy who has not grown up but still thinks like a child. What worked for you before, will not work for you any longer. It is time to grow up.

You may have had many good ideas and perhaps you even put some of those ideas into place, but it is time to let them go now. So the first step on this voyage on which we are traveling, makes a stop at the altar. It begins with you laying on it every plan for ministry that you have ever had.

Until you can let go of those visions, the Lord cannot do anything with you. He cannot lead you in a new direction and if you want to spend another year in the garden pulling out weeds, then hold on to your visions! But if you desire to enter into the fullness of all that the Lord has for you, then it is time to let them die.

Apostolic Preparation 1st Marker

Chapter 09 – Apostolic Preparation 1st Marker

If you have had children, you will be able to look back on their lives and mark their progress. You will recall the time that they cut their first tooth and the first step they made without holding on to anything.

You might recall their first day at school and then as they got older, you will recall their first date. If you have older children, you will remember their wedding day and the birth of their children. And so you can walk through the events of the past again and mark the changes and growth in them.

As you head out in your apostolic calling, you will begin as your child did when they cut their first tooth. Then as you press on through and endure the preparation and training to come, you will become a spiritual adult, in the same way they learned to stand up for themselves and face the world alone.

And so in the same way that you can mark the progress of your child's growth and the stages they passed through, so is it possible to mark your own spiritual growth and the stages of maturity that you will pass through in your apostolic calling. There are clear markers along the way that will tell you where you are and where you are headed in your calling.

All That Good Advice

Remember how much good advice you had for your own children as they grew up? They may have taken your advice, or they may have ignored you, yet you still had been where they had not been before. Having faced the rigors of adolescence yourself you could help them face theirs. Only as they became adults, did they realize that "mom and dad" knew what they were talking about. Now they get to pass all that advice on to their own kids!

There are so many Christians that would benefit if they would only take the time to learn from others! The Lord is resurrecting mentoring and apostolic fathering in the Church today for this exact purpose. And simply by receiving the counsel and direction of one who has gone before you, you have an advantage that so many others did not.

So allow me to take your hand now as I point those markers out to you and let you know where you are in your apostolic preparation and what lies ahead of the road. As you go through the various phases of apostolic preparation you will be amazed to discover that the Lord has had His hand on your life all along to shape and mold you into the vessel He has called you to be.

What is Apostolic Preparation?

The educational system is something that all of us are familiar with. You have come to understand that if you want to succeed in anything in life, that you have to gain a bit of knowledge first and that you have to qualify.

When you go to see a doctor or a specialist, you expect that he was trained and qualified in his field. You would certainly not place your life in the hands of a person who was not properly trained would you? Well preparation and training for ministry is the same thing.

As an apostle, you are like a surgeon who will be called of God to heal, restore and sometimes even apply the scalpel to the lives of others. Now just as you would not entrust a loved one into the hands of an unqualified specialist, so also the Lord cannot entrust His people into your hands if you have not qualified.

Some people have this crazy notion that because they did not succeed in anything in the world that all they are qualified for now is to be a minister for the Lord. This ideology is a fallacy, because the opposite is true. The Lord requires a greater commitment and qualification than the world!

The Lord requires that you excel in all the tests and preparation that He presents you with and He has a full curriculum in mind for you also. So before you can stand up and boldly proclaim that you are an apostle, there are a few tests that you will need to face and a few things that you will need to learn.

Someone aspiring to be a surgeon would need to register in a university and gain enough credits to pass. He would have to work hard and only years later would he have the privilege of calling himself a doctor. Only when he finally attains that doctorate does he know what he is and what he is capable of.

So as an apostle in preparation, you might know that you are called, but only once you have qualified will you really know what you are and what you are capable of. This is what apostolic preparation and training is all about.

Apostolic Preparation is the longest part of the whole process and can last up to 40 years. These years are phase after phase of being stripped down and having everything removed from your life that would hinder your calling.

I have said this before and I will say it here again to labor my point, **"Apostolic preparation is learning how not to do everything. Apostolic Training is learning how to do everything right."**

Apostolic preparation is phase after phase of being stripped down to nothing, while apostolic training is a phase of being built up and added to.

So what exactly is the standard for apostolic preparation? What is it all about and what can you expect? The Apostle Paul laid it out perfectly for us in this passage:

> *1 Corinthians 9:19 For though I am free from all men, I have made myself a servant to all, that I might win the more;*

20 and to the Jews I became as a Jew, that I might win Jews; to those who are under the law, as under the law, that I might win those who are under the law;

21 to those who are without law, as without law (not being without law toward God, but under law toward Christ), that I might win those who are without law;

22 to the weak I became as weak, that I might win the weak. I have become all things to all men, that I might by all means save some.

What Does Preparation Entail?

Apostolic preparation will take you to the heights of elation and to the depths of despair, yet in that tumult you will undergo a process of change and metamorphosis. I just shared a passage with you from 1 Corinthians where Paul shared the preparation that he had to go through for the calling. He had to become all things to all men.

He had to become weak and strong. He had to become as a Gentile and a Jew. He had to become a servant and a master. Those sound like contradictions, don't they?

That is why the apostle will lose his identity in Christ, because Christ was all of these and only in Christ will you attain to any form of perfection.

By Colette Toach

The Four Markers of Preparation

So let's get practical again and apply this to you and to your life. How can you identify the preparation of the Holy Spirit in your life and what further preparation can you expect?

As you continue along the markers that I will lay out for you now, I want you to mark each one off that you have lived and make a note of those that you have not. You will not qualify for apostolic training until you have fully completed each of these phases in your preparation.

1st Marker: Ministry and Denomination Preparation

The person who makes the best kind of employer in the business world is the guy who worked his way through the ranks. There is nothing worse than being employed by someone who inherited the company or who was given his position because he was family!

The kind of person where everything fell into their laps make the worst bosses, because he never understands his employees. He has never been where his employees are and so he cannot relate to their struggles or their positions.

This kind of boss is dominating and usually expects more out of you than you are able to give. Have you ever had to work under someone like that? They are difficult people to get along with and it makes working under them a very unpleasant experience.

Then sometimes, if you are blessed, you will get the opportunity to work under someone who has been where you are. They can identify with what you are going through and also have a good idea of what to expect from you – because they have been there. They worked their way from the basement up and know every level and position of that business.

This kind of person makes the best boss and he automatically has the loyalty of those under him. He is respected and loved, because people know he understands!

This is the kind of leader that the apostle has to be and it is also one of the reasons why his preparation is so intense. Before an apostle can put a foundation together, he has to work his way up the ranks a bit first. Paul also faced his share of working through the ranks and even after he returned from Arabia, he was not immediately set apart for the apostolic office.

First he had a bit of learning and living to do!

> *Acts 11:25 Then Barnabas departed for Tarsus to seek Saul.*

> *26 And when he had found him, he brought him to Antioch. So it was that for a whole year they assembled with the church and taught a great many people. And the disciples were first called Christians in Antioch.*

After having his time in obscurity Paul still had to operate in various ministry capacities and so he joined Barnabas in Antioch and helped him to establish the church there by teaching and pastoring the people.

You will read later on how he shares with Timothy the correct pattern for leadership and how the elders are to conduct themselves. How did Paul learn all of that? He learned it through experience. Paul had worked through the ranks so to speak and as a result could make the demands he did of those who then came under his care.

You too will be made to experience various ministries and the Lord will cause circumstances to come upon you in apostolic preparation that will take you from one ministry type to the next.

You may begin taking care of the babies in the nursery, then on to the youth group to the intercessors group and then on to being church treasurer. With each change though, you are learning the 'ins and outs' of the church system and its strengths and weaknesses.

Fivefold Ministries

Your ministry preparation does not end there however and you will also face the additional preparation and training for each of the fivefold ministries.

If you are to be an apostle who will be putting each fivefold ministry into place in the church, then you will be required to understand each of those ministries!

I remember watching a documentary once of a composer and how he put musical scores together for various shows. The one thing he said really stood out to me.

He said, "I have to be familiar with every single instrument in the orchestra, while I do not play every single one, I do know what each one is capable of and where it fits in my arrangement."

And so the apostle is like a composer who will need to put everyone in their place to create a perfect harmony. However before he can do that he has to learn what each ministry is capable of. So as part of your preparation you will learn how to operate as a prophet, as a teacher, pastor and evangelist.

You should be able to identify each of those phases in your preparation and if you cannot identify a time where you trained in each of those, then make a note of it now for that is where you are headed and it is indeed the first stage you will go through before being taken to the next marker.

To help you identify if you have worked through each of the fivefold and what they entail, I recommend *The Fivefold Ministry Series*.

Denominations

It takes a special kind of person to begin something from scratch and to build up a business with very little resources. You cannot help but respect someone who had nothing to begin with except the shirt on their back and a dream in their hearts.

But if you had to go and speak to anyone that has ever been successful you will learn that things did not fall into their laps. You will find out that before their great success that they faced many disappointments and saw many of their plans fall around their feet. Yet with persistence and determination, they finally came to the place where they reached a breakthrough and began to build something substantial.

Apostolic preparation will encompass many 'hit and misses' and you might even come to the place where you are asking God what exactly He wants from you, because you seem to be going in a different direction to everyone else and then failing and having to change direction again.

If you are called to be an apostle, you will find yourself shifted and shunted through many different kinds of churches and denominations. The Lord will lead you into a church that does not believe in the move of the spirit.

Then again, He will lead you into a church that does not emphasis the Word much. With each direction that you go and with each time that you try to 'make it' in these churches and fail, you are learning a very important lesson. You are learning what the Church as a whole looks like.

A businessman does not make himself successful by being narrow minded. No, by launching into many different arenas, he gains an understanding of the whole business industry and it adds to his wisdom and ability to make better plans.

Surveying the Land

Just imagine for a moment, a builder who wants to build an apartment complex. Would that builder not first survey the land and make sure that it is suitable? Would he not find the best place to build the complex? This is exactly what Nehemiah did when he was planning to rebuild the walls of Jerusalem:

> *Nehemiah 2:11 So I came to Jerusalem and was there three days.*
>
> *12 Then I arose in the night, I and a few men with me; I told no one what my God had put in my heart to do at Jerusalem; nor was there any animal with me, except the one on which I rode.*
>
> *13 And I went out by night through the Valley Gate to the Serpent Well and the Refuse Gate, and viewed the walls of Jerusalem which were broken down and its gates which were burned with fire.*

Before he even set his hand to building, he first surveyed the land and saw what kind of materials were needed and what it would take to put the structure into place.

Now as an apostle, God is going to call upon you to build His End Times Church and how will you build it unless you have surveyed the land? Just as you would think a builder foolish for trying to erect an apartment complex without first seeing the layout of the land, how much more would you be foolish to try and implement the mandate that God has given you without first getting a full overview of the condition of the Church?

In the Secret of Night

If you take a look at Nehemiah, you will see that He took the initiative to survey the ruins and then set his heart to putting a plan together to bring about their restoration.

Notice that he went in the silence of the night to survey them and in the secret of his own chambers he sought the face of God as to what He should do.

So will you as an apostle be sent into obscurity and be taken by the Holy Spirit to many different churches and denominations so that you might come to see and understand the condition of the Church.

Because until you can see the damage and what needs to be done, how can you go about restoring anything? This explains why the apostle spends so much of his time in obscurity. It is in the secret of the night and in the solitude of your prayer closet that you will begin getting your apostolic mandate from God.

Only then will you be ready to include the many others who will be able to help you put those walls up! Just as Nehemiah put together the resources and the plans for the building of the walls after he had received a full picture of what he was to do, so will the Lord also release you to begin building your own pattern and plan.

The building of this pattern will begin in surveying the land and learning a few lessons in ministry. This and more is what you will come to see as the apostolic preparation in your life.

My Personal Experience With Denominations

I began this learning experience from as far back as I can remember! Although I was brought up primarily as a charismatic Pentecostal, the Lord was not content to leave it at that.

At one time we got involved in a Baptist church and this was the second church that I played the drums for. I learned some important lessons on the pressures that come along with leadership.

And so although I was young, it did not deter others from pointing out that I was playing way too loud and that the traditional music that they were accustomed to was not what we were playing!

Right back here I came to understand that the majority of the Church does not like change and that once their templates are threatened that they can become rather uncomfortable! I had to learn how to overcome this situation and keep my peace. Sometimes I managed to cope, other times I did not.

Later on I ended up joining a girls group that was associated with a Methodist church. In order to join the group, I had to join the church. I was a teenager at the time and I remember my friends and I sitting at the back of the church timing the prayers, just wishing that the service was over already!

There were many other churches that God led us to and from the most liberal Pentecostal church to the most staid Methodist church I came to learn that God does not favor the one over the other and that His plan includes them all.

I came to understand that His End Times church will consist of every believer and that if he loves them, so should I.

So where are you at? Can you identify this preparation in your life? What did you learn? Let's take a quick look now at our apostolic types and how they endured this kind of preparation.

David's Preparation

I can imagine how excited David felt to be anointed by Samuel, yet little did he know what he would have to endure. The first task that David was given was to play music for Saul. After that he was called upon to be Saul's armor-bearer.

Then later as he overcame Goliath, David got the opportunity to be placed in charge of a legion of soldiers. By the time that David left the courts of Saul, he had learned everything he needed to know about being a king and running a kingdom!

David and Saul are also perfect examples for my illustration of the boss who had everything handed to him and the boss that worked his way through the ranks. Saul had the Kingdom handed to him on a silver platter, so to speak, and as a result never understood the people.

Saul was neither loved nor respected by the people and was forced to make threats to get them to follow him. Why do you think this was? Simply put, Saul had never been where the people were.

David was so different. He had worked his way from the sheepfold to the throne and as a result could identify with the people at every level. The people adored David and gladly gave their lives for him.

In fact all he had to do was whimsically mention that he desired some water from the well at Jerusalem and three of his mighty men risked their lives to get it for him. That is how much David had their love and loyalty.

And so you have a choice today as well. You can submit to the storms of preparation and be humbled to work your way through the ranks or you could be as Saul and try to do it through natural means.

It all depends what kind of leader you want to be. Do you want to be a David or a Saul? It is up to you, but it does come with a price.

Moses' Preparation

At first glance you would say that Moses had it easy! He got to live it up in the palace of Pharaoh while his fellow Israelites suffered in slavery. Yet if you take a look at his life you will see how Moses also got to work his way through the ranks, just having a different starting point to David.

Moses is a good picture of an apostle who is within the church system and is called of God to rise up into apostleship. The first thing that happened to Moses is that he ended up leaving Egypt.

And so if you are one who has held leadership positions in the world and in the Church, you will find that with the call to apostleship will also come a phase of being thrust out of those positions to hide in the wilderness.

It was in the wilderness that Moses learned a thing or two about being a leader. He, like David was left with the sheep and although he had learned all about being in the courts of Pharaoh, he learned now how to serve his father in law.

So no matter where you are and from what vantage point the Lord calls you from, you will be called to experience the many levels of leadership before being placed as an apostle.

By the time God had given Moses the pattern he was known as a prophet, as one who spoke to God face to face and a teacher of the law.

Joshua's Preparation

Very little is told of Joshua's past and as he rises out of obscurity you notice immediately that he never left the side of Moses. Joshua was to Moses as what Elisha was to Elijah. He was disciple and servant. Everywhere that Moses went, Joshua went also and along that journey he got to glean from the experiences of Moses.

So if the Lord raises you up through a spiritual father, there is still no escaping this preparation! You will need to learn all there is to know and you will likely live it through your spiritual father.

You will get to do all the jobs that he does not want to do. It says in the scripture that Elisha washed the hands of Elijah. In other words, he did all the dirty work.

If the Lord has placed you under the fatherhood of another apostle and you find yourself in the background doing all the jobs that he does not want to do, then rejoice. It is part of your preparation.

Solomon's Preparation

Solomon was like Joshua, in that you hear very little about him until he was ready to take the throne. At first you think that Solomon had it made. He just got the throne handed to him. But if you take a look behind the scenes, you will see that it was not true.

Firstly Solomon nearly lost the throne a few times and then when he finally got it, he needed David to show him what to do. Solomon did not remain ignorant, because David spent time with him, teaching him what to do and how to care for the people. Solomon did not just take the throne and remain exalted above the people.

If you read the scriptures, you will note the account of the two harlots who came to Solomon with their babies. *1 Kings 3:16 Now two women who were harlots came to the king, and stood before him.*

Solomon allowed these harlots into his court to hear their case. He did not hide himself from the people, but instead came down to where they were and asked the Lord for the wisdom to judge them.

This is the mark of a true apostle and one who will be respected and will bring the Church into her final glory.

Apostolic Preparation 2nd Marker

Chapter 10 – Apostolic Preparation 2nd Marker

2nd Marker: Personal Preparation

I remember having a conflict with someone once where they were airing their opinions concerning my lack of tact. They found my abruptness to be offensive and confronted me with it. At the time I was quite indignant and replied, "This is just the way God made me and you will have to accept me the way I am!"

Now that sounds really politically correct and at the time I thought it was a pretty good come-back, but as time went on I came to discover that this was not the way "that God made me" and that not even the Lord was willing to "accept me just the way I was!"

After we had been married for a few years, Craig and I looked back over our life together and noted the many changes and transformations that we had gone through. As I looked at him I realized that he was no longer the man I had married and as I looked at myself, I came to see that I was not the woman he had married either.

And for that I thank God! Imagine if we remained the same immature couple we had been when we were newlyweds? As the Lord had taken each of us and began to transform us we were conformed more to His image.

Not Good Enough to "Be Who You Are"

Apostle in training, "being who you are" is not good enough for God and it is not good enough for God's people.

The flesh is full of sin as Paul says:

> Romans 7:18 For I know that in me (that is, in my flesh) nothing good dwells; for to will is present with me, but how to perform what is good I do not find.
>
> 19 For the good that I will to do, I do not do; but the evil I will not to do, that I practice.

Do not think that because you have certain temperamental traits that it is good enough to remain in them. Just as you had to experience each of the fivefold ministry, it is also vital that you experience and move into each temperament.

Four Main Temperaments

The apostle in essence is a jack of all trades and different tasks require a different temperament. Now I am not going to get into detail here as to the various temperaments because I cover them in extensively in our schools and other materials.

However, I will mention that there are four in particular and they are: The Expressive temperament, the Driver temperament, the Analytical Temperament and the Amiable temperament.

You need to identify the various phases of change that the Holy Spirit will take you through to shape your character.

Paul says: *1 Corinthians 13:11 When I was a child, I spoke as a child, I understood as a child, I thought as a child; but when I became a man, I put away childish things.*

A babe in Christ might be able to get away with "the way he is" but as an apostle you are not allowed such a privilege. If you take a look at the life of Jesus you will see how He rejoiced when it was time to rejoice and wept when it was time to weep.

The Father had full control of his emotions and his mind and will. So also you will be asked of the Lord to give him your mind, emotions and will.

If you are overly emotional, the Lord may require you to be solemn in a certain situation. If you are overly solemn, the Lord will ask you to be expressive. I have seen this in personal experience when ministering to different cultures.

Some cultures are open with their emotions and to reach them you need to match that emotion. While other cultures are more withdrawn and hide their feelings, and so to be all things to all men, so that you might save some (as Paul says) you will need to hold your emotion back.

The ability to function in all four temperaments will make or break your ministry! Now you are going to find that your temperament will be addressed more in the workplace than anything else.

If you do not like to mix with people much and are an analytical that would rather be behind a desk, planning and figuring things out, the Lord will cause you to go into a profession like sales to teach you how to handle people and to gain the ability to follow things through.

If you are the kind of person that thrives on a challenge and is totally goal orientated, like the expressive temperament is, then the Lord will put in you in a position where you have to endure a daily routine where your emotions are brought into subjection and your zeal into order.

If you are the kind of person who never finishes a job he starts and could spend all day talking to people, like the amiable temperament is famous for, the Lord will cause you to work in a situation where you are forced to confront people and be more assertive.

Then again if you are the kind of person who is a good organizer, is the leader and is the one who makes the decisions, like the driver temperament is, then the Lord will cause you to sit under the leadership of someone else and to be a servant, thus handing your control over to them.

Now in each of these cases, it does not seem like a lot of fun, but as you submit to those changes and allow yourself to be changed, there is not a single situation or a single person that you will not be able to handle in ministry. This will likely take the bulk of your preparation as it digs deep into your character and personality make-up.

So can you identify the change in your life? Take a look at your life and try to remember what you were like when the Lord first called you to ministry. Then take a look at yourself now. Can you see the changes that you have gone through?

Can you see now, how right before your eyes a metamorphosis is taking place without you even realizing it?

All Things to All Men

Now that you have a picture of the kind of changes that you are going to face in your personal life, how do you think these changes will come to pass? The Holy Spirit is very innovative and you will come to see how He will use anything at His disposal to mold you into the apostle that He has called you to be!

We have come to find however that the Lord will often use your family and work situations to bring about these changes. I gave you a few examples already how the Lord will call someone who is not really people oriented to go into a job that will require them to mix with people.

When someone says to Craig and I, "I didn't know that you could 'cook' or 'fix cars' or 'design graphics" we will answer them by saying, "Hey, I'm an apostle! I can do anything!" This little phrase of his began as a joke, but it is so very true!

I discovered this as I looked back over my journey. When I first left school I ended up as a waitress at a local steak house. Not a very high calling is it? I cannot begin to tell you how many lessons I learned concerning people though. Of course this was the same place I met my darling husband who was a waiter at the same restaurant! (God really does have His hand in all you do!).

After Craig and I were married, I ended up spending some time as a nursery school teacher. Training and taking care of children from ages 2 through to 6. Here I learned many lessons on patience and strangely enough on leadership.

To this day I still swear, that if you can lead a bunch of kids all going their own way, then you could lead anyone!

Then a little later the Lord opened the door for me to go into the catering business where I learned many natural skills that included cooking, hosting, business and how to fare for myself.

The Lord was not done with me yet and opened the door for Craig and I to get involved in the computer industry. I can proudly say that I know how to put a computer together from scratch!

Since then the Lord has led me into so many different realms. From learning to cut hair, write books, graphic design and set up websites.

Now if you take a look at each of those job situations, you will note how none of them are similar. Only in later years did I come to see God's plan in it all. I not only learned natural skills that are now allowing me to set up the infrastructure for the ministry that God has given me, but it also dealt with my temperament and exposed all my temperamental weaknesses!

This learning has not stopped and the Lord continues to lead both Craig and I into different arenas. It stretches us, it changes us and it also helps us identify with others. May we never stop learning and growing and becoming all things to all men!

It is exciting to see progress where you thought you failed, isn't it? But press on because we are not done yet. So how about our apostolic types? Can we identify their temperaments and the changes they went through? See if you can figure it out for yourself and then compare notes with my conclusions.

David's Temperament

Without a doubt David was an expressive! He was emotional and was always opening his big mouth when he should have kept quiet. When he went to see his brothers on the battlefield and saw Goliath, he viewed his opinions quite openly!

He displayed his emotions openly in dance before all the children of Israel. He wept openly at the loss of his son Absalom and was openly angered at those who said they had slayed Saul.

David thrived on a challenge and a goal. He was a hero in the battlefield, because when he set his hand to something, he always finished it.

To bring David's expressive nature to death, the Lord led him to the cave of Adullam. Here all his goals fell around his feet. All his plans and hopes were brought to death and instead of being able to go out and do everything he wanted to do openly, he was forced underground.

We begin seeing a transformation in David when he has the opportunity to kill King Saul. What a different person we see now compared to the hotheaded shepherd boy on the battlefield with Goliath.

Where before he was shouting up a storm at Goliath, here you see David tip-toeing around Saul to pick up his water jug and spear.

By the time David reached the throne, he knew when to show his emotion and when to hold it back. He had truly learned to flow with the heartbeat of God and so can you if you will allow the Holy Spirit to change and shape you.

David was also a man of many talents. He was a warrior, a shepherd, a psalmist, an inventor and a dancer! That is quite a list. But not only did David conquer the nations around him with an arm of steel, but He also invented a whole range of new musical instruments and then trained the singers to worship before God!

This was a man of many talents and a perfect candidate to fulfill the mandate God had given him.

Moses' Temperament

Moses was not a very confrontational kind of person and at the first sign of trouble he ran from Egypt. Moses was an analytical temperament and this is very clear when God calls Him by appearing in a burning bush and all that Moses could do was ask questions.

This is so typical of the analytical temperament. You tell an analytical what you want to do and he will give you ten reasons as to why it will not work!

This was Moses right down to his boots and God had to really get tough with him to pull him into line! Eventually to shut him up God said to Moses, now beginning to get angry with him" *Exodus 4:11 So the Lord said to him, "Who has made man's mouth? Or who makes the mute, the deaf, the seeing, or the blind? Have not I, the Lord?"*

Moses was so afraid to step out and confront that the Lord had to give him Aaron to speak on his behalf. But by the time Moses and the children of Israel were ready to leave Egypt, Moses had gone through a transformation.

Instead of the analytical we saw before, we see a driver, expressive temperament coming out of him when he says hotly to Pharaoh,

> *"Exodus 11:4 Then Moses said, "Thus says the Lord:'About midnight I will go out into the midst of Egypt;*
>
> *5 and all the firstborn in the land of Egypt shall die, from the firstborn of Pharaoh who sits on his throne, even to the firstborn of the female servant who is behind the handmill, and all the firstborn of the animals.*
>
> *6 Then there shall be a great cry throughout all the land of Egypt, such as was not like it before, nor shall be like it again.*
>
> *7 But against none of the children of Israel shall a dog move its tongue, against man or beast, that you may know that the Lord does make a difference between the Egyptians and Israel.'*
>
> *8 And all these your servants shall come down to me and bow down to me, saying, 'Get out, and all the people who follow you!' After that I will go out." Then he went out from Pharaoh in great anger."*

Now that looks like a very different person to the one that questioned God on the mount and you too will see the same transformation in your own life through the trials of apostolic preparation.

Joshua's Temperament

Now Joshua was as opposite in temperament to Moses as you could get! Where Moses was the analytical, Joshua was the Driver and was the kind of person that if he saw an obstacle, he would just bash through it! Joshua was very impatient and quick to anger.

Consider this passage,

> *"Numbers 11:27 And a young man ran and told Moses, and said, "Eldad and Medad are prophesying in the camp."*
>
> *28 So Joshua the son of Nun, Moses' assistant, one of his choice men, answered and said, "Moses my lord, forbid them."*

Joshua was hotheaded and this is one issue that got him into a lot of trouble when he made a treaty with the Gibeonites in disobedience to God's commandment. He too faced some change as the Lord worked on him and as he put aside his explosive nature, he learned to settle and divide the land that God had given them.

He had to portion everything out and bring the plan of Moses to pass. The plan that Moses had left behind was very specific and Joshua did not have the option to change it or suddenly go his own way.

By Colette Toach

Instead he had to follow his orders and the pattern of someone else. His control and what he wanted to do bowed to what God wanted and as a result the children of Israel occupied the Promised Land. And so if you are willing to relinquish your control to the Lord and become a servant, He will shape and change you into the leader he has called you to be!

Solomon's Temperament

Every time I read anything about Solomon I think to myself that he was such a nice guy. Solomon was not overly emotional. You do not see him running in different directions. He was consistent and he kept a good order.

However as David passed the throne on to him, he left Solomon with a full list of jobs that had to be done. None of them were easy jobs either!

In some cases David requested that he put certain people to death like Shimei who had cursed David.

> *1 Kings 2:8 "And see, you have with you Shimei the son of Gera, a Benjamite from Bahurim, who cursed me with a malicious curse in the day when I went to Mahanaim. But he came down to meet me at the Jordan, and I swore to him by the Lord, saying, 'I will not put you to death with the sword.'*
>
> *9 Now therefore, do not hold him guiltless, for you are a wise man and know what you ought to do to him; but bring his gray hair down to the grave with blood.*

Now that does not sound like an easy job for a nice guy. And so after David died instead of putting Shimei to death Solomon allowed him to live under certain conditions. Well I am sure you could have guessed that Shimei disobeyed those conditions and Solomon had to have him killed in the end.

It was not easy for Solomon but through the confrontations he was forced to face he overcame his weaknesses and from being the nice guy, he rose up to being a strong leader. And so you will likely face times when you will have to confront people or do things that you do not want to do.

When this happens, then rejoice, for it may not be pleasant but it is changing and molding you so that you will be a fitting vessel for the Lord's purpose.

Apostolic Preparation 3rd Marker

Chapter 11 – Apostolic Preparation 3rd Marker

3rd Marker: Social Preparation

I came to a stark realization after having been appointed to apostolic office that when you reach this level of authority that there is no such thing as a "personal life." I came to realize that there was not a single thing that was not in His hand and not under His control.

From the intimate moment with your spouse to how you want to raise your children, there comes a realization that wherever you are, that the Lord is in your midst and in control of the situation.

Often you think that you have missed God or that you have disqualified yourself from the calling because of your mistakes, but if your heart still beats for the calling in your life, regardless of what you have done, then the Lord will continue to mold and shape you for that calling.

As I agonized over the many weaknesses I saw in myself that still needed to be dealt with, the Lord said to me "You have more faith in your ability to fail, than you have in my ability to raise you up."

This statement has remained with me and each time I feel that I am not attaining or being the leader I think I should, I remember those words. His ability to change you is greater than your failure, and His ability to prepare and train you is greater than your blindness to see His work in your life.

From the most insignificant struggle in your life to the most dramatic one, God is in control and in those events He is shaping and changing you continually. So let's press on to see how the Holy Spirit prepares and changes you as a person, as a believer and most importantly, how He changes you into a leader fit to wear the title 'Apostle' for Him.

Gender

I suppose that by being a woman that I would be considered to have a disadvantage in ministry. It is no secret, that there are many in the Church today who feel that a woman cannot hold apostolic office.

Strangely enough though this thought had not occurred to me until it was brought up by someone. I had always followed hard after the calling on my life and I grew up in a home where my father made it clear that anything was possible in the Lord.

He never put any spiritual restrictions on me. And so at the age of 13 I was the drummer for the worship band at church. At 14 he helped me structure my first little sermon and I stood up to preach it with knees shaking, but with strong convictions!

I remember that first lesson my Dad gave me on homiletics. He was not the kind of Dad who cared a big deal about grades or what sports we did at school, but that day I saw him beam from ear to ear as I stood up for the first time in his shadow.

Little did I know how much I would use those principles later in life.

It was in one of our times of intercession that I saw the Lord Jesus for the first time and got my ministry call. Dad was excited as he explained what it meant for me. He simply forgot to add that bit about, "Well as a girl, of course, you will need to be careful and forget about taking any of this stuff seriously ..."

In his eyes I could take on the world if I wanted to. And so it was the same in mine.

So not once during this time did it occur to me that my gender should stand in the way of my calling. Although my father affirmed my femininity, it was my potential for ministry that he cultivated the most. And as he did, I grew from strength to strength.

Only after I had been in prophetic office for a season and was in the throes of apostolic training did someone say to me, "Don't you think that it is difficult to be a prophet or an apostle when you are a woman? Don't you find that you get a lot of opposition?"

This statement baffled me for a bit. For the first time in my ministry I was confronted with a truth I had not considered before... I was a woman! How could I have missed that?

By Colette Toach

When I stood to minister I had never thought of myself as a woman before. I listened to the heartbeat of God and went where He said go. I received what God spoke to me and just did it with the naiveté of a child.

Now to you I might sound ignorant and perhaps a little too naive, but I have come to realize that it was this very naiveté that saved me. The reason being, that because no one took the time to tell me that I could not do it, I just did it with blind obedience and touched God.

Now there are many times I am asked the question, "Do you believe that a woman can be an apostle?" to which I could give you a full study and argument, but such an argument is usually fruitless and only ends in strife and ill feelings.

So if I am asked a question like that by a woman, I would say, "If you still notice your gender when you stand to minister, then you are nowhere near ready for the apostolic calling on your life. God does not minister through gender, He ministers via the Holy Spirit, manifesting through your spirit and there are no 'men and women spirits', just willing vessels."

Until you can forget your gender, you are not ready to be an apostle. God does not call men or women. God calls willing vessels and He will use a donkey, as He did with Balaam to speak to His people if He has to. Well, I just happened to be a suitable donkey for the Lord at the time and so He used me.

To a man asking me the same question, I would avoid debate again and follow Paul's advice in 1Timothy 4 (below) and say, "I do not find offense that you do not believe I can be an apostle as long as you do not find offense when God uses me!"

My apostleship does not lie in what I call myself, but in what I am. Which leads up to our next point perfectly.

> *1 Timothy 1:4 Nor give heed to fables and endless genealogies, which cause disputes rather than godly edification which is in faith.*
>
> *5 Now the purpose of the commandment is love from a pure heart, from a good conscience, and from sincere faith,*
>
> *6 from which some, having strayed, have turned aside to idle talk,*
>
> *7 desiring to be teachers of the law, understanding neither what they say nor the things which they affirm.*

Culture and Titles

We had a dog once that acted just like a cat. It would pounce and play with a ball of yarn, just like a cat did. But do you know something? It was still a dog and nothing it did could change that fact.

When it opened its mouth it barked like a dog and when you looked at it, you could see that it was a dog – no matter how it acted. If I tried to insult my dog and say, "you are not a dog, you are a cat!" it would look at me dumbly and not really care much, because it was …what it was!

So what does this have to do with apostolic preparation? When God has called you as an apostle, you need to come to the place where you know who you are.

Just like that dog, you could say what you liked to it, but it did not change what it was and it did not change the way it barked and stood.

If you are still being offended by people that do not believe in apostles or refuse to recognize your apostleship, then you are nowhere near ready for training.

The reason for this is that you do not know what you are yet. Does it really matter if people believe that you are an apostle, when you are one? Does it really matter what they say, when you stand up and speak like one?

But the greatest problem we have in our church society is that **we rely too much on titles and too little on the anointing and authority given by God**!

I believe that our fruit should speak for itself and to be honest, I am too busy doing the work of God to get side-tracked by someone not believing that God can't call a woman to be an apostle.

If I am an apostle and have a mandate, does it even matter that I have the title or not? Do people even have to know? If I am invited to minister to a group that did not believe in woman apostles, it would be both arrogant and sinful of me to impose my title upon them!

For such a group, I would come without my title "apostle" and I would still minister as an apostle, without them knowing it. What is more important? The title, or the ministry of an apostle?

To use my illustration, I might try to be a cat and act like a cat, but underneath I still look and act like a dog! Taking the title away does not change who I am!

If you are being invited to speak at a church or in a denomination that does not believe in apostles, then just go as a minister of Jesus Christ and do what He tells you to. Then you will leave having ministered as an apostle and having spoken as an apostle and having acted as an apostle ...without them even knowing it.

Who cares if they know or not! The only thing that should matter to you is that you are doing what God wants you to do. Now if this is something that you are finding hard to do, then you are nowhere ready for apostolic training yet and need to face the fires of preparation for a season.

Just as I was appointed to apostolic office the Lord said to me, "Are you willing to know that you are an apostle, but to never wear the title or let anyone know? Are you willing to stand in the highest ministry office and be considered nothing special?"

What a price it is to put in all the effort and give your life, without receiving the recognition for that purpose. This was a tremendous death that I faced and only when I was prepared to submit to it and remain in secret, did God begin to raise me up in His timing and in His way.

God will raise you up when you are ready, but until you are willing to lay your apostleship at His feet and your need for recognition, you will not qualify to stand in His place and speak to His people.

Race and Culture

Whenever I see someone standing up and berating others for being racist, I cringe knowing that they are not confident in who they are in the Lord. The issue concerning races and culture is very much like the issue of gender.

I have come to notice that when you see your race as a hindrance in your ministry, so do others! I remember sharing with a lady minister once and she was relating how she received so much opposition from men in ministry who would not receive her.

I had to confront in her, her own bad image. Because she felt insecure as a woman, others treated her accordingly.

I have had some opposition being a woman, but no less than other men in the same situation. Why the difference? Because being a woman is not an issue for me, it is not an issue for others either!

Now the same applies to race and culture. When race and the color of your skin is an issue to you, then it will be an issue to others as well. When you feel inferior and feel that you are at a disadvantage because of your race, then you will be at a disadvantage.

I love to look at the illustration that Jesus used of the good Samaritan. A man went on a journey and was robbed and left for dead, yet the only man who was willing to help was a Samaritan!

Now in those days a Samaritan was considered abhorrent to the Jews. No one would want to associate with a Samaritan. I tell you what though, that dying man did not care very much who that Samaritan was when he was carried on a donkey to an inn and fed and healed.

I am sure that as the Samaritan picked him up that he did not say, "Hey! You can't help me! You are abhorrent to me! I am not supposed to let you touch me!" No, that half dead man was only too grateful for the help!

Today things are no different. People are dying in the Church and you have what they need to live. Now when you bring healing and minister to their needs, they will not care much who or what you are, they will only see their restored life.

Now if you are going to get all hung up on your race and the color of your skin, then you are going to miss God. God does not see in color and neither should you.

This is a subject that is rather extensive and one that I have discussed with many people of different cultures. I am blessed with being able to reach many different nations and as a result have come to speak to many people of different races.

However, each time I discuss this issue it is the same. For those who grew up unaware of any racial difference and just went on their normal life, they shared with me how they did not find that they received any rejection due to their race.

On the other hand, I found that those who were insecure concerning who they were, were often rejected. So who needs to change here? The people of God? The world? No, you need to change and you need to see through God's eyes before you will be ready for ministry.

At the end of the day, it is about doing the work of God and doing it with His anointing and His ability. And until all that you see is Jesus when you look into a mirror, you will remain ineffective and unable to complete the mandate that He has given you.

Age

It has been exciting to see how the Lord is raising up the new generation to take His church into the new era. If there was one thing I struggled with as I began to wade in the waters of ministry, it was my age...or lack thereof as the case may be!

Having received the calling so early, I found it difficult to fit in with the adults and difficult to fit in with the kids.

My age seemed to stand against me more than anything. It is true, people are not willing to receive from someone that has not lived a little ...or so I thought.

The Lord really tested this place of insecurity in me when He began leading me to help with our prophetic school. I was only 23 when I was placed in prophetic office and began mentoring and training the prophets.

For the longest time I felt insecure and ill-equipped for the task. However, I came to yet another startling realization. I came to see that when you met the needs of God's people and flowed in the anointing, that they did not notice your age. God began teaching me a powerful lesson on His ability and His strength versus my inability and my weakness.

I came to see that He delighted in using the weak and foolish. And so the Lord began to show me that the fire

By Colette Toach

that had burned in me from the beginning was of Him and that He could use me.

Growing up I had always desired to see children rising up to their full potential in the Lord, but not being allowed to.

As an adult I passed this heritage on to my own children and as children they get to minister the truths of the word and flow in the spirit. Not because of who or what they are, but because of who Jesus is and His ability to anoint.

Never forget apostle in preparation that it is in your weakness that Jesus is glorified and it is His anointing that makes you what you are.

There is no greater hindrance than the hindrance in your own mind and in your own insecurities. And so apostolic preparation will work upon those fears and insecurities and conform you until you come to the place of being able to minister to anyone, anywhere and with the anointing that is needed, without your own issues getting in the way.

Finances and Class Distinction

As an apostle in preparation you will learn as Paul did,

> *Philippians 4:11 Not that I speak in regard to need, for I have learned in whatever state I am, to be content:*

12 I know how to be abased, and I know how to abound. Everywhere and in all things I have learned both to be full and to be hungry, both to abound and to suffer need.

Because, once again, you need to reach all men for Christ. If you are insecure next to someone of good repute or who is wealthy, then your word will be compromised.

Neither Jesus nor Paul were moved by the rich or poor. They did not feel insecure next to those that had power and fame and they were not moved by the beggars and the blind. They ministered to both equally.

Content to Abase and Abound

Now depending on which side of town you are, you will learn to live both the flourishing and the lacking that Paul speaks of here in Philippians chapter 4.

If you were brought up in a wealthy home and had your needs met, you are very often blind to the needs of others. Because your needs were always met, you cannot understand why others are struggling and why they cannot just pull themselves out of it.

It is a common human error to think that because something comes easy to you that it should come easy to others. I learned this in a very revealing conversation. The person I was talking to had a real problem with talking in front a group of people and showing their emotions openly.

Now being demonstrative (and somewhat emotional) it is very natural for me and I find it comfortable standing and speaking in front of others. I was getting frustrated with this person's arguments and struggles as they tried to explain that they just could not stand up and speak like I did.

I said, "It's easy, you just stand up and open your mouth and God will give you the confidence you need. All you need to do it to take that step!"

I could not understand their fear, just as much as they could not comprehend my blind boldness. I would like to think that I have grown up a bit since then, but the principle here is the same as with financial lack.

If you always had everything handed to you on a silver platter, you cannot understand people that have to fight for every penny they get. For you, it is easy to generate finances.

So what does God do with you? You may, as Paul did, find a time when the finances do not flow as easily as they did before.

Now is this God's way of punishing you or trying to make a point? Not at all, it is part of your apostolic preparation and it will enable you to minister effectively.

Preparation in Prayer

I remember the hard time my stepmom went through when she married my father. She grew up in a home on the better side of town, where she did not know lack. If she needed something, it was always there for her.

Her apostolic preparation started with a bang the day she met our family! Well, you have to give my dad some credit. He did issue this warning to her the night he proposed, "I want you to know, that if you marry me, things will not be easy for you. You will have to fight for everything you have. People will turn on you. But together we will do the work of the Lord."

Certainly the most unique marriage proposal I have ever heard of. It must have been love, because not only did she marry him, but she stood by his side 100%.

For the first time in her life she faced lack and had to learn to live by faith. She was a trooper though and took it in her stride. It was during this time that she learned so many of the prayer principles that became the core of her ministry.

To this day, if there is one person in the family who has the faith and ability to push through in prayer concerning financial lack, it is her. She learned to do it by living through it first.

Without that lesson she would never have been able to relate to others who did not have her upbringing.

By Colette Toach

Neither would she have the spiritual authority now to deal with this problem in the lives of others.

Only when you have been where others are, can you relate to them. Only when you have learned to be content when you abound and abase, will you be effective for the Lord.

All your prejudices against folks who are poor will be addressed, until you see all believers with the same eyes, whether male or female, black or white, rich or poor.

Overcoming Poverty Mentality

Now do not think that if you grew up on the poor side of town that you do not need to change your templates either! In fact, I would say that you will likely face more dealings if you grew up poor than if you grew up rich.

Why is this? Wealth is a strength and poverty is a weakness and if you know anything about ministry preparation, you will know that confronting your weaknesses is always more difficult than dealing with your strengths.

Now I was the poor kid in town. In South Africa, where I was schooled, all the schools had their own uniforms for the students to wear. I have shared already how we used to move around a lot and because of that we always had to get a new uniform according to the school we went to.

But as you can imagine, being poor, my parents could not always afford to get me brand new uniforms every time we moved. So in the end we had to go to what they called the 'Swap Shop' to try and find second hand clothing that would fit. Boy did we hate that!

Often I had to take a size or two larger than I was, because it was the only size available. It was tough enough to go to a new school, without standing out with a uniform that was hanging badly on my skinny shoulders.

Then there was a time when the economy took a very bad turn and my father was retrenched. To help out, the school put us on a program that enabled us to be fed at school. Each morning they would provide us with breakfast and at lunch they would give us something from the cafeteria.

Now that might have sounded like an admirable thing for them to do, but the humiliation was sometimes worse than the hunger! I remember once being called out of class by a teacher to come and have breakfast.

As a kid, I felt so humiliated! When I came back all the other kids in my class wanted to know why I just didn't have breakfast at home. I was labeled the "poor kid".

By Colette Toach

So as you can imagine, these events started to develop insecurity in me. Even worse than that, they developed a poverty mentality in me.

Because I had always known lack it restricted my view of ministry. Because I was used to everything being beyond my reach, I never tried to reach for anything!

When the Lord gave me a task I would respond with, "Oh no Lord, I could never afford that!" Even after the Lord gave us principles for success and we broke free of that terrible lack, I still held on to that same poverty mindset.

And so I came to learn that you can take a poor kid out of poverty, but that it would not remove the poverty mentality. Only the Holy Spirit could do that and He did it by confronting my weakness head-on! For those who have known wealth, the Lord will cause them to know lack.

But for those, such as myself, who had a poverty mentality, what do you think the Lord does?

The Lord will cause you to come into contact with those who are wealthy and successful. So God began exposing this weakness in me by sending me people who were very wealthy and capable, to minister to and to socialize with.

Slowly He eroded at my fears and insecurities. I came to see that we are all one in the Lord Jesus and that when I looked through His eyes, I saw the same hurts in those who were wealthy as those who were poor.

Not only did the preparation cause me to see people through the eyes of God, but it also took away my poverty mentality and replaced it with possibility thinking!

Possibility Thinking

Where before I would not move forward because I felt we could not afford it, I was now going ahead and making plans without having the money in the bank, just because God said so.

I no longer feared lack and learned to confront it. I overcame it with the power of the Holy Spirit and suddenly what was impossible in my mind before was now possible and God reigned instead of my fear!

If you are bound with a poverty mentality, then this will be smashed before you are ready for what God has for you. Your limited vision clouds the fullness of what God has.

Apostolic preparation takes away your fear of trying to reach the stars. It opens up your spiritual vision to see the sky and to imagine that you could grasp a star in the palm of your hand. If you are not at that place of thinking and believing big, then allow the Holy Spirit to complete the preparation in you.

By Colette Toach

Then again, until you can understand and relate to those who have had lack, you need to come down to earth a bit and relate to others. You need to become all things to all men, so that you might save some.

Spouse and Family

God is raising up apostolic teams in the New Move and you will find that these teams consist mainly of families that He has brought together. You just need to look through the old and new testament to see how God has used families and continues to use them!

Your family is no different and if there is one principle you need to keep in mind with regards to your family, it is this: The day you were called to the apostolic ministry, your family was called along with you.

I said at the beginning of this chapter how nothing is personal anymore and that there is not a single thing that God does not get involved with. Well your marriage and family life are no exception.

Consider this passage,

> *1 Timothy 3:2 A bishop then must be blameless, the husband of one wife, temperate, sober- minded, of good behavior, hospitable, able to teach;*

> *3 not given to wine, not violent, not greedy for money, but gentle, not quarrelsome, not covetous;*

> *4 one who rules his own house well, having his children in submission with all reverence*

> *5 (for if a man does not know how to rule his own*
> *house, how will he take care of the church of God).*

Now why do you think Paul gave such strict conditions for someone called to minister? Because not only are your family a part of your ministry team, but they will make or break your ministry!

A good marriage will be your rock on stormy seas and your children will be the ones to will carry your heritage to the next generation.

Unfortunately, this is not how the family unit is seen in many ministries. There needs to be a change in the way we see things as leaders and as apostles in the Church.

Your spouse and your children are those that will take your ministry to the next generation. In fact if I want to see the real condition of a person's spiritual life, I only need to look as far as their family. Your children and spouse will reflect who and what you are.

The Exceptions

Now it is not always as straight cut as that and there are times when a spouse or a child goes their own way and will refuse the calling given to them. It is then that you will find yourself at a crossroads.

You see, you cannot rise up into apostolic office and have your house out of order. Your spouse and you are one flesh and the Lord's anointing will flow through you both.

By Colette Toach

There are many who married and later discovered that their spouse would no longer support their calling. So what are they to do?

Now this is a subject that can cover a book all on its own, so I am not going to get into much detail here. The bottom line is that God has not called you as a person, but He has called you as a family and the sooner you see that, the sooner you will rise up into all that God has for you.

If your family does not want to follow that calling, then God may remove them, but never take that into your own hands. God will ordain who He ordains and He will remove who he removes.

If you place your life in His hands, He will take care of all of these details, right down to the smallest matter.

Paul says it well in,

> *1 Corinthians 7:13 And a woman who has a husband who does not believe, if he is willing to live with her, let her not divorce him.*
>
> *14 For the unbelieving husband is sanctified by the wife, and the unbelieving wife is sanctified by the husband; otherwise your children would be unclean, but now they are holy.*
>
> *15 But if the unbeliever departs, let him depart; a brother or a sister is not under bondage in such cases. But God has called us to peace.*

16 For how do you know, O wife, whether you will
save your husband? Or how do you know, O
husband, whether you will save your wife?

Paul did not say here, if your husband is an unbeliever and does not support your ministry then leave him. No he says that if he wishes to remain, to allow him to remain. It is up to God to remove any spouse that stands in the way of your ministry.

God honors the commitment of marriage whether you married in Him or not and will seek first to woo your spouse. They are partakers of your anointing and your calling!

If after they refuse to yield to his wooing, He will remove them in His timing and in His way. Your responsibility is to seek after the things of God and to include your family!

It is your responsibility before God to identify the potential in your spouse and children and to make everything that God has given you available to them. Before you will even embark on the first step of apostolic training, your marriage and your family will need to be in order.

Apostolic Types

Let's move on quickly now to our apostolic types and see how they fared in their training.

David

I see a lot of these signs of preparation in the life of David. David certainly learned how to abase and abound. David grew up in a fairly wealthy home. His father had enough clout to send David directly to the commander of the army with gifts, when David's brothers were in battle against the Philistines. Yet David also knew the sheep pen and having to work hard.

Just a little while later David gets to 'live it up' in the courts of Saul and overcomes any poverty mentality. Then later is sent to the cave and the wilderness where he learns to be content even when he has nothing! When David finally took his place upon the throne, he could relate to the people and could also act like a King, for he had lived them all and had learned to be content in any situation!

David also had to let go of his family heritage and race when he had no choice but to remain with the Philistines. He was also forced to leave Michal, the daughter of Saul when he fled. He paid all for the call and only later do you see how God had his hand in that, for Michal only proved to be a hindrance to his Kingship.

David also had his age to overcome and you see an incredible progression from Shepherd boy to warrior by the time he had left the courts of Saul. David never allowed his age to stand in the way of his calling and by the age of 27 took the throne of Judah.

Moses

Although Moses was born in a poor home, he lived in the palace of Pharaoh and knew wealth all his life. He could not relate to God's people in slavery and could not understand why they did not try to free themselves.

Forty years in the wilderness changed Moses and so he learned to abase and to abound in all things. This certainly prepared him for the hardship that he would yet face in the long years of wilderness wanderings to follow.

Moses left all behind and when he and his wife Zipporah got into conflict concerning the circumcision of his sons, he sent her back to her father and went on to Egypt alone. Only later when he returned to the mountain did Jethro bring them back to him.

> *"Exodus 4:25 Then Zipporah took a sharp stone and cut off the foreskin of her son and cast it at Moses' feet, and said, "Surely you are a husband of blood to me!"*
>
> *26 So He let him go. Then she said, "You are a husband of blood!" - because of the circumcision.*

Moses also had his age to deal with and was completely opposite to David and Solomon! He was an old man when he began his ministry and there are many today who are in the same boat.

It would seem that the years have passed you by and you feel like your life is wasted. But if you would see how much Moses accomplished when he had passed his prime, you will see how God has His hand in all things.

There are many who share with me that they feel that they missed God or took up the calling too late in their lives. This is not true, because the calling is God's and He will use even your failures to His advantage.

The Lord is still calling many Moses' today, who are no longer young. Had Moses gone to Egypt too soon, he would have missed God's plan and so the same applies to you.

God has a plan for you and you are in His perfect time. So do not be discouraged, but realize that your life has indeed been a phase of one preparation after the next and even if you have been in the desert for 40 years, that it was perfectly timed in God's economy.

Conclusion

Can you see how the Lord has been using everything in your life to prepare you? He will use your family and He will use your work situation. He will use pastors who reject you and He will use ministries who will oppose you.

In fact, each time that you received a wall in your face, thank Him, for it was His tool to shape and change you. I think that this scripture just sums up this chapter perfectly,

> *Romans 8:28 And we know that all things work together for good to those who love God, to those who are the called according to His purpose.*
>
> *29 For whom He foreknew, He also predestined to be conformed to the image of His Son, that He might be the firstborn among many brethren.*

In every situation you find yourself and in every failure and weakness you have, God will indeed be glorified and it is in your weakness and in the melting pot of affliction that you will begin to see the face of Jesus being reflected in yours. So submit to the fire for when it is the hottest, is when you will experience and display His Glory!

By Colette Toach

Apostolic Preparation 4th Marker

Chapter 12 – Apostolic Preparation 4th Marker

4th Marker: Leadership Preparation

The Progression From Child to Leader

As we have looked at the various stages of preparation I think that the most intense phase of them all is the preparation one has to face when your ability as a leader is challenged.

It is a common misconception that an apostle is a 'natural born leader.' Well if this was the case then Paul really missed it when he said,

> *1 Corinthians 1:26 For you see your calling, brethren, that not many wise according to the flesh, not many mighty, not many noble, are called.*

> *27 But God has chosen the foolish things of the world to put to shame the wise, and God has chosen the weak things of the world to put to shame the things which are mighty,*

The Most Foolish

So let's make one thing very clear here before we get into this chapter. God chose you for one reason and one reason alone: You were the most foolish, most weak and the one most incapable. He looked at your weakness and said in His heart, "This is a perfect candidate to illustrate my grace and glory."

How would it glorify God if you were able to do it without Him? It is so tempting to look in the world at those who are successful and say, "If only they would get saved, what a tremendous tool they would be for God."

You could not be more wrong! God is not looking for those who are 'wise after the flesh' but rather those who are weak and foolish, so that He might be magnified through them.

God delights in taking an impossible situation and turning it around for His glory. How many times did the Lord say to Israel, *Isaiah 49:3 And He said to me, You are My servant, O Israel, In whom I will be glorified.* If your desire for ministry is to glorify your own name and to have others look at your success then you will never reach apostolic office, because you have taken the call of God into your own hands.

By the time you rise up into full apostolic office, it will be the name and face of Jesus Christ that will be glorified through you. You will stand in awe and look at what you were and what you have become and you will know that it was indeed the work of the Master who conformed you.

Then as others look at you and your weakness and see the strength of Christ in you, they will also glorify God because of what He has done in your life!

If I look at my own life, there is nothing that I can boast of that would give me any merit in this world or in the Church. But the Lord looked down on the weak and useless vessel I was and said, "I can work with that!"

Why has God chosen me and why does He use me? Because I am so clever or because I am so spiritual? No, He chose me because I was available and foolish enough to be picked up, dusted off and shaped by His hand.

What a Leader is Not

And so we come to the last phase of apostolic preparation. It was an exciting day the Lord revealed His will to me and told me what He had planned for me. He showed me how He would raise me up as a leader, to stand as a model for others. How wonderful that all sounded! Boy was I in for a surprise.

Just days after receiving this word, the Lord began to show me what a leader is NOT! I made every mistake that is possibly known to man with regards to leadership. I upset people, I made wrong decisions and then when I thought I could not possibly mess up one more time, I messed up some more!

My delusions of grandeur flew out the window in lighting quick time as I came to realize that being a leader was not as easy as it looked and that I was very far from being the kind of leader that God wanted me to be.

By Colette Toach

I always believed that the definition for a leader was simply: A person that others follow. But I came to realize that the standard for leadership in the world is not the same standard in the Kingdom of God.

After having been in ministry and having been a part of the executive team, the Lord decided at that point to show me what a lousy leader I was! What? But Lord can't you see how successful I am? Lord I helped to build this ministry! I have people from all over the world coming into our training schools and under my mentorship, how can you say that I am a lousy leader? I made it didn't I?

How arrogant and blinded I had become. And what a startling reality it was for me to discover that God's approval of my calling did not depend on how wonderful I thought I was, but rather on the price I was willing to pay.

Well maybe by the world's standards I had made it, but in the eyes of God I had just begun. There is more to being a leader than just building a ministry from the ground up. When I taught the Prophetic Field Guide Series, I taught on the various levels of prophetic ministry.

I teach that there are the sons of the prophets, who function in prophetic ministry. They speak prophetic words and were quite a large group in the Old Testament. Then you have Elisha who through mentorship, rose up quickly into prophetic office. Then there is Elijah who is trained directly by God and mentors the "Elijah's".

According to the level that you desire to reach as a prophet, the price for the calling will differ. If you are satisfied to remain a "sons of the prophets," then you can be happy to face a small amount of death and only give up some things.

But if you desire to reach the higher level, then the price will be greater... it will cost you everything.

Now that principle also applies to the apostolic ministry. And Paul says it so well here, *2 Timothy 2:20 But in a great house there are not only vessels of gold and silver, but also of wood and clay, some for honor and some for dishonor.*

There are various levels of apostolic authority and you could be content to just remain a pastor or a leader over one little ministry and be satisfied with your portion. Or you could be divinely discontented and ask the Lord for everything He has for you. You better know this though: that desire comes with a price.

That price would it be to admit that maybe you have not arrived yet and that you need to become a true leader. What kind of vessel you will be, is up to you. Do you desire to be a vessel of gold or a vessel of wood?

By Colette Toach

Growing up!

Are you ready to admit that you have some growing up to do? To aid me in this lesson, the Lord gave me an interesting passage,

> *Matthew 5:3 Blessed are the poor in spirit, for theirs is the kingdom of heaven.*
>
> *4 Blessed are those who mourn,*
>
> *For they shall be comforted.*
>
> *5 Blessed are the meek, for they shall inherit the earth.*
>
> *6 Blessed are those who hunger and thirst for righteousness, for they shall be filled.*

He told me that for as long as I was "poor" and "hungry" and "meek" He would continue to make me rich, feed me and give me the nations. Because when you think you are full, then what need do you have of food? If you are rich, then why should God bless you?

However if you continue to hunger and look at yourself saying, my leadership is poor! My ministry ability is poor, I have so far to go! Then God can continually strengthen you and raise you up.

The minute you become lifted up in your own eyes and say, "My belly is full and I am satisfied with my good life and successful leadership." Then you hold back the hand of God in your life and you will never get to taste the milk and honey of the Promised Land!

If you could admit that you are a child and then climb up on the knee of your heavenly father, you will inherit the Kingdom of Heaven. The Lord will honor your weakness and your innocence and He will raise you up.

You just need to have your heart open to receive and the Holy Spirit will give you one great portion after another. Never be satisfied with what you have apostle in training!

Even when you reach apostolic office, never become satisfied! Hunger and thirst, cry out to God and be meek and in your thirst He will give you living waters and for your hunger He will continually give you the bread of life.

May you never become content with your portion and may you never be satisfied with what you think you have. May you always reach forth for a greater measure and a deeper understanding of God and as you reach out even now with all that is inside of you may you touch the hem of Jesus and be restored, healed and lifted up in the eyes of God and in the eyes of man.

Child Versus Adult

Now that you have learned what a leader is not, you are well on your way to change and growth. God began to challenge you and expose all your weaknesses and it is also likely that He exposed all the wrong images you had of leadership during this time.

As a child you look around you and make judgments on what you think a leader looks like. Then as you grow up you begin imitating those who you think are good leaders.

It is a natural course of life that every person that you admire and look up to, you imitate. And so you are conformed to their image. Now this is a good principle in the case of scriptural parenting and mentorship, but there comes a time when you must become unique in your calling and mandate.

It is a painful thing to admit sometimes that everything you are is actually based on someone you looked up to as a child.

So think back on everyone that you admired as a child, an adolescent and then as an adult and see if you began taking on their image. If so, then this is where you need to start breaking free. You are to be formed to the image of Christ, not the image of man.

So why do you have to let go of your past mentors? Well firstly, it is important to remember that a mentorship relationship is always temporary. Secondly, you have grown up a bit since then.

Especially when it relates to spiritual mentorship. When you first got saved you did not have the relationship with the Lord that you do now. You could not hear Him for yourself. So you needed a mentor to represent the Lord for you. You needed that mentor to show you how to relate to the Lord and even hear the Lord's voice for you.

You needed to learn those lessons on submission and servanthood. It was a time in your life where God shaped you through that relationship. However, you have grown up since then and hopefully you can hear the voice of the Lord for yourself now.

Spiritual Childhood: The Transition

So there comes a time in the life of every disciple when he reaches the same level as the mentor and has to move on. There comes a time when you can see God for yourself and speak to Him for yourself. It is at this time that you need to break all mentorship ties and be conformed to the image of Jesus!

> *2 Corinthians 3:18 But we all, with unveiled face, beholding as in a mirror the glory of the Lord, are being transformed into the same image from glory to glory, just as by the Spirit of the Lord.*

You are conformed ... from glory to glory! From one image to the next. This is not a once off thing. It is a continual process. And so as you let go of the old, you will embrace the new and so begin to be conformed to the image of Jesus Christ.

Now this transition from being a disciple to being a mentor is like the transition of a child becoming an adult.

Spiritual Adolescence

Do you remember that painful time in your life called adolescence? Do you remember all the struggles and frustrations you faced? If you were anything like me, a lot of the struggles you faced were with your parents!

Suddenly they just did not understand you! You had so many plans and ideas and they seemed to keep holding you back. And so you sought to go out and find your own path.

This is a very difficult phase in the life of any person, but so important, because out of that adolescent will rise an adult who will set the pace for the next generation.

Now the apostle in training is very much like that adolescent and has many lessons to learn. But just like an adolescent thinks he knows better than his parents, so also does an apostle in training feel that he already knows all there is to know.

You and I both know that only when you became an adult, did you discover how little you knew about life!

I discovered this little lesson in my drumming. I had played the drums all of my life and had come to the place where I was quite happy with the way I played. I became content with how I played. But what really happened is that I had put myself into a rut! I felt that I had learned all that I needed to learn and so I did not grow.

Then one day the Holy Spirit walked into that area of my life and revealed that I really did not know much at all and that I needed to break out of my rut and go to the next level. And so after 15 years of playing drums, I came to this stark reality that I actually knew nothing! The more I learned the more I realized that I was ignorant.

This is a perfect picture of you in preparation right now. You might think that you know a few things and that you are pretty good at what you do, but as the Holy Spirit comes into those areas of your life, you will discover that you in fact know nothing!

Do not despair, because that is a wonderful place to be. In fact, it is a sign that you are beginning to enter into adulthood!

Spiritual Adulthood

What marks an adult? I have had the opportunity to watch my own children grow up as well as my brother, who is quite a bit younger than me.

As I watched him grow up, I saw that as a child he always tried to get out of cleaning his room or doing anything that his mother wanted him to do. Why do all that boring stuff when you could play all day?

Then came the day when he learned some responsibility and the importance of being part of a team. He learned that he could no longer allow everyone to do everything for him. He could not take being carried for granted and so he learned to do things for himself.

At first it was just picking up his socks. Next it was disciplining himself to take out the trash without being nagged. After that it was helping out by shrink-wrapping books in the publishing division of the ministry. Soon enough though he was pulling his weight as a team member and taking on a managerial position.

Then one day I observed the difference between him and my own children. I noticed how I would really have to be firm with them to tidy their room or do any other household tasks. I noticed that John never had to be asked twice to do anything. If he said he would do a job, you could consider it done.

It was clear. My baby brother had grown up! He was beginning to mature.

So the first sign that you are making it past spiritual adolescence is that you are beginning to take responsibility for your own actions. You are cleaning behind yourself, so to speak and God does not have to nag you to do His will, because you do it without a fight.

When you make a mistake, you are willing to admit your failure and ask for forgiveness. When you have a responsibility, then you take up the task on your own shoulders and do not try to pass the buck or get away with it.

Do you think that my illustration is too simplistic? It is shocking how many spiritual babies there are behind the pulpit, who think they are adults, but have yet to reach adolescence!

Saul was such a baby and when God told him to do something as simple as destroying the Amalekites in their entirety, not only did he disobey God and keep the spoil, but when Samuel confronted him, he blamed the people!

This is a clear sign of an immature leader and one that is not fit to lead the people of God. Only when you can come to the place of taking responsibility for your own actions and being obedient regardless of your feelings, are you ready for the next phase of leadership training.

Spiritual Leadership

So how do you know when you have finally reached the place of adulthood? I remember when it first struck me that I was no longer a child and could no longer get away with the things I did before.

Craig and I were settled in our first home and I enjoyed setting up our home and beginning to get into a routine of my own.

By Colette Toach

A while later our firstborn Deborah-Anne came along and everything changed! Along with this little bundle came a whole new routine and I suddenly found that the time I had to myself, was no longer my own. Craig and I did not have the same kind of freedom anymore and could not be as spontaneous or be as socially active as before.

While I was cleaning out Deborah's room one afternoon, I looked down at her sleeping in her crib and it suddenly hit me. I am not a child anymore. I am a parent now. I was not just responsible for myself, but I was also responsible for this little stranger that had come into our home.

Craig and I were no longer "a couple" but we were a family now. Not only did we have to carry our own cares and needs, but also the needs of this child and then later on the three other children that followed.

Now in this simple illustration you can define a leader. A leader is someone who not only takes responsibility for his own actions, but of the actions of others as well. I think that Paul is such a good example of this in scripture.

> *Philippians 1:3 I thank my God upon every remembrance of you,*
>
> *4 always in every prayer of mine making request for you all with joy,*

5 for your fellowship in the gospel from the first day until now,

6 being confident of this very thing, that He who has begun a good work in you will complete it until the day of Jesus Christ;

7 just as it is right for me to think this of you all, because I have you in my heart, inasmuch as both in my chains and in the defense and confirmation of the gospel, you all are partakers with me of grace.

Paul carried the burden of his churches continually in prayer. He did not birth them and then leave them to their own devices. No, rather they were in his heart continually and he did not cease from caring for them and taking the responsibility of their success and failure upon his own shoulders. This is the true mark of a leader.

Taking the Blame

Remember the illustration of the businessman who worked his way through the ranks and one who inherited his position? We knew a woman who was the kind of boss who had worked her way up from the typing pool to be the manager of her whole division.

I heard this story about her. One day she received a call from her superior. As it turned out one of the reps in her division had misquoted a client and it had ended up costing the company money.

Instead of reacting badly to the situation and putting the blame on the rep, she took the full brunt of the blame upon herself. She answered, "I take full responsibility for that and I apologize." Even though it was a rep that had made the error, as the leader she took the responsibility for him and took the blame.

If you look at that illustration it reminds us of what Jesus did for us on the cross. He took our blame on Himself. When he was strung up on those wooden beams and the Father turned His eyes from Him, did Jesus say even once, "But it is not fair! It was not my mistake! It was not my sin?"

No, He took our blame, even when He had done nothing wrong.

If you want to be as Jesus and so represent Christ to His people, then it will mean becoming a true Shepherd like Jesus was. Being a leader means taking responsibility for those who are in your care.

It is so tempting to look at someone who has failed and to blame them and turn away from them. But a true leader would take the responsibility on his own shoulders and see what he could do to rectify the situation in love.

Passing on the Heritage

I got my own conviction on this one when I was facing a lot of struggle with the kids. They seemed to be going through a stage of rebellion and would not listen to a word I said.

I was at the point of tearing my hair out by the time I came to the Lord and asked for direction. His reply was very pointed, He said, "If your children are out of order, then your own life is out of order, because the Word says, *1 Timothy 3:4 not given to wine, not violent, not greedy for money, but gentle, not quarrelsome, not covetous; 4 one who rules his own house well, having his children in submission with all reverence 5 (for if a man does not know how to rule his own house, how will he take care of the church of God?)*

That convicted me and brought me to repentance. I realized that my children were simply picking up the conflict I was facing in my own life and were reacting to it. I came to understand very well that your children will not do as you say, but will do as you do! Now this lesson does not just apply just too natural children, but applied to those you mentor and spiritually parent as well.

Depending on your spiritual condition, those who are in your care will act accordingly. So if they are in rebellion, would you dare look for that rebellion in your own life? If your flock is out of order, are you in order?

If your flock lacks faith, do you have faith? If your flock lacks love, do you have love? A mature leader is someone who is prepared to look at his own beam first to enable himself to take the spec out of his brother's eye.

To be this kind of leader you need the kind of confidence that will give you the ability to take this kind of responsibility. While you are insecure and are too wrapped up in your own weaknesses, you will not have the strength to overcome your own failures or the failures of others.

And so this chapter on leadership preparation is just a foretaste of what we are going to discuss and that is, how to become a leader like Christ.

It takes more than just knowing what a leader is to change. It requires the loving hand of the Lord to come on you and to shape you into that image. So submit yourself to the Lord and give Him license to change you and to shape you.

Because when you submit to His loving and firm hand, the images that you were will pass away and reveal the image of Christ, changing you from glory to glory.

Let's see how our apostolic types fared in their leadership training!

David

The transition of David is the clearest of all the apostolic types! David was only a child when he tended his father's sheep. Right there he learned to take responsibility for his own actions and also for the lives of his sheep.

When a bear and a lion came along to devour the sheep, he rose up and killed them. He did not leave the sheep to bear or lion, but rather put his own life at stake for theirs. This was indeed leadership training for David, as soon he would be the leader of God's people.

After that you see David being made a captain over a thousand men. Here David learned to be a leader again and be faithful. However, the strongest test of David's leadership was in the cave of Adullam where every scoundrel came to him. What a difficult bunch they must have been to handle.

You see such a difference in David the shepherd boy and David the king. He started out a bit arrogant and sure of himself, to becoming a mighty warrior and then sitting on the throne as one who was in control and admired by the people.

None of this came easy to David though. He had to pay the price of giving up everything before he reached that place just as you will also be asked to pay the price for the call.

Moses

Moses really had a lot to learn about leadership having grown up in the courts of Pharaoh. It does not mean that because you are given a position of leadership that it makes you into a leader!

By Colette Toach

Although Moses had grown up in a place of privilege, none of it taught him how to lead God's people. Once again this proves that there is no such thing as a 'natural born leader' in the Kingdom of God. God makes leaders with the molding of His hand and He does it in a way that no one would anticipate.

Instead of placing Moses in a position to lead his people, he sent him out to the backside of the wilderness. It was here that Moses learned to be a leader and to become a vessel for God. He lost his own delusions of grandeur and after a humbling and learning to submit to his father in law and care for the goats, only then was he ready to go back!

What a change we see in Moses as he led God's people. When God wanted to slay them for sinning, Moses defended them and interceded on their behalf!

> *Exodus 32:10 Now therefore, let Me alone, that My wrath may burn hot against them and I may consume them. And I will make of you a great nation.*
>
> *11 Then Moses pleaded with the Lord his God, and said: "Lord, why does Your wrath burn hot against Your people whom You have brought out of the land of Egypt with great power and with a mighty hand?"*
>
> *12 Why should the Egyptians speak, and say, "He brought them out to harm them, to kill them in the mountains, and to consume them from the face of*

the earth'? Turn from Your fierce wrath, and relent from this harm to Your people."

And so you might have been given positions in the world or in the Church. Maybe you were like me and grew up in a Christian home and were always involved in the Church. Does this make you a leader? It makes you just as much of a leader as it made Moses in the courts of Pharaoh!

Positions do not make a leader and recognition by man does not make a leader. Only the Holy Spirit can forge a godly leader and this is why you as an apostle in training will endure the shaping and death to the flesh required to conform you.

Joshua

Joshua learned how to be a leader under the fatherhood of Moses. He began as a servant and did all the jobs that Moses did not care to do. It is likely that he was Moses body guard as he followed Moses everywhere and protected him. Only when he had qualified as a servant was he ready to become a leader.

And so perhaps the Lord has you under the fatherhood of another man or woman of God. Are you willing to submit and just be a servant? Are you willing to follow their mandate and fit into their plans? As you prove yourself in servant hood, only then will you qualify to become the leader that God has called you to be!

Solomon

Solomon was not much of a leader when he took the throne, but he got off on a very good footing when he asked God, "*1 Kings 3:9 Therefore give to Your servant an understanding heart to judge Your people, that I may discern between good and evil. For who is able to judge this great people of Yours?*"

He knew that he was just a child and could not lead God's people. Yet as he allowed the Lord to give him wisdom, he changed from being afraid to confront, to wielding the sword and enlarging the borders of Israel.

If Solomon, who became the richest man of his time could admit that he could not lead without the miraculous intervention of God, then how much more you and I? To be a leader according to the world's standards will only get you so far.

It will take a miraculous transformation to equip you to be the kind of leader that is going to change the face of the Church.

Are you willing to let go of your natural abilities and natural leadership skills?

Remember, Paul said,

> *1 Corinthians 2:5 That your faith should not be in the wisdom of men but in the power of God.*

6 However, we speak wisdom among those who are mature, yet not the wisdom of this age, nor of the rulers of this age, who are coming to nothing.

7 But we speak the wisdom of God in a mystery, the hidden wisdom which God ordained before the ages for our glory,

The wisdom of man and the wisdom of this age will not give you the power of God. No amount of learning and studying will make you a leader or give you the power of God.

Only by submitting to the cross in your life and yielding everything that you deem as a credit in this life will open the door to you experiencing the power of almighty God in your life!

Before proceeding to this next chapter, may you say as Paul, *Philippians 3:8 Yet indeed I also count all things loss for the excellence of the knowledge of Christ Jesus my Lord, for whom I have suffered the loss of all things, and count them as rubbish, that I may gain Christ.*

CHAPTER 13

Stepping Out
Into the Apostolic

Chapter 13 – Stepping Out Into the Apostolic

Early in my prophetic ministry the Lord gave me a vision to gather all the prophets in a network to mobilize them to speak forth the direction that the Lord had for the Church at any given time.

I began with great gusto and felt that this was the full vision that the Lord had given me for ministry. How devastated I was when right at its peak, the Lord told me to hand the whole operation over to someone else and to step aside.

What was going on? I had birthed it, I had trained up the prophets in the network. I had spent hours ministering and raising them up. Then just when the fruit had begun to form, the Lord told me to give it all up.

Did the Lord not think I was capable to finish what I had begun? The Lord knew something that I did not. He knew that if I stayed behind to enjoy just that portion of fruit, I would not move on to produce further trees that would yield their own form of fruit.

An Orchard of Fruits!

When I was growing up there was a period of my life when we lived on an acreage. As a child I thoroughly enjoyed all the fruit trees in that place! We had apricots, plums, peaches, apples, grapes and plenty different garden vegetables.

Summer was the best time of year and we would feast on all that fruit as kids! I can imagine that if there was only one kind of fruit tree on that acreage, summer would not have been quite as exciting, but we had a whole selection to choose from!

Imagine if the only tree that grew were plum trees. You can only eat so many plums and then you have had enough! The Prophetic Network that I had founded was like a plum tree. And while it bore good fruit and was a great tree, it was not enough.

The Lord wanted a greater variety for my ministry. What I thought was my final destination was in fact just the starting line for me.

Stepping Into the Apostolic

Well my first little sapling is no different to any other church or ministry that has been founded in times past. Anyone can start a church and make it bear fruit. Any leader who has a pastoral ministry has the anointing to gather the flock together and form a congregation.

And many have been confused, thinking that the sign of an apostle is someone that starts ministries. Even in the New Testament you will note that the church at Antioch was founded by ordinary leaders and that Paul and Barnabas had to be sent there as the apostles to establish it!

Take a look at this:

> *Acts 11:20 But some of them were men from Cyprus and Cyrene, who, when they had come to Antioch, spoke to the Hellenists, preaching the Lord Jesus.*
>
> *21 And the hand of the Lord was with them, and a great number believed and turned to the Lord.*
>
> *Acts 11:26 And when he had found him, he brought him to Antioch. So it was that for a whole year they assembled with the church and taught a great many people. And the disciples were first called Christians in Antioch.*

Philip also founded a church in Samaria, yet in scripture he is known as an evangelist and not as an apostle. In fact the Word says that:

> *Acts 8:14 Now when the apostles who were at Jerusalem heard that Samaria had received the word of God, they sent Peter and John to them,*

Philip may have had what it took to begin a church, but it took the apostleship of Peter and John to establish the work. In Antioch ordinary believers began that church simply through their zeal and testimony. So it takes a lot more to being an apostle that just starting a few churches.

What sets the apostle apart is that he is one who is not only able to begin a work, but is also able to raise others to maintain it and then move on to another piece of land to produce another fruit tree.

Smashing a Sacred Cow

So let me smash a sacred cow right now. For those who think that to be an apostle means to start churches, it would be like saying that someone who plants a tree is a gardener! Someone can plant a tree in the garden to make it look good, but it does not make them a professional gardener.

No. A gardener is someone who not only knows how to plant a tree, but knows how to make it grow, helps it produce fruit and then teaches others how to tend that tree, as he moves on to plant another one in the garden.

He lives, breathes and thinks gardening. It is something that he does every waking moment and not just when the fancy grabs him.

If you are looking for a pastor who has an apostolic ministry, then begin by looking for someone who not only started his own ministry and succeeded in birthing it, but has also raised up others in his church to tend it.

Then that same pastor would have established a pattern and given everyone a place to function in it. When you looked at his ministry you would not just see one type of fruit, you would see many. You would also see many gardeners helping him tend to that fruit!

Down to Grass Roots

Craig grew up in a family that enjoyed gardening immensely and each year they would trim and prune their yard, adding lots of different plants each season. Their garden did not consist of just one kind of plant.

They planted ferns in the shade and daisies in direct sunlight. In summer their garden was a whole blanket of colors and different textures. Imagine how boring it would have been had they just planted ferns everywhere!

This picture illustrates a distinct difference between someone called as a pastor and someone who is called as an apostle. Someone called as a pastor will continue to plant the same shrubs.

He will build the same foundation over and over again. Each plant will look the same. Now there is nothing wrong with that, the Church needs pastors! Just like a garden needs many blades of grass, the Church needs pastors to keep sowing and building!

The apostle is not content with just one grass patch after the next. As I have shared before, the apostle is always changing and a good sign that a pastor is in fact apostolic is the fact that he begins reaching beyond the realm of his previous influence.

He begins building works that have a variety of functions and bear a variety of different fruits. This is what sets the apostle apart and what makes him unique!

As a pastor, he may birth many churches that have the same operation and function well and bear much fruit. But when such a pastor steps beyond his original foundation and begins planting ministries that reach different kinds of people and have a different orientation, be sure that such a pastor is called to be an apostle and is in apostolic preparation.

This is very true of the Apostle Peter who said to his fellow pastors,

> *1 Peter 5:1 The elders who are among you I exhort, I who am a fellow elder and a witness of the sufferings of Christ, and also a partaker of the glory that will be revealed:*
>
> *2 Shepherd the flock of God which is among you, serving as overseers, not by compulsion but willingly, not for dishonest gain but eagerly;*

Here Peter clearly states that he too is the elder of a local church. He puts himself among the other pastors scattered in Asia.

Do a quick study of the ministry of Peter and you will note that he founded the New Testament church, opened the door for the gentiles and traveled many places instructing the church in the apostle's doctrine.

When Jesus called Peter he asked him to tend His sheep, and while he began with the small group of 120 on the day of Pentecost, his ministry exploded in many different directions after that, reaching different people and bearing various fruits!

Tending the Garden

Now if I get back to my illustration of the gardener, you will notice that once a gardener has planted a tree, he does not leave it to the elements to take care of itself. No, he keeps checking on it.

Then as his garden increases, he will enlist the help of others to help him out. He will come back to take a look at that garden to mark its progress. If the tree is not yielding good fruit, then he would tell those whom he enlisted for help, to tend the tree and add fertilizer to its soil.

If the tree was overgrown, he would give instructions for it to be pruned. If he had to leave that tree to the elements. It would end up growing wild and the fruit on it would dwindle to become small and bitter.

So the gardener is diligent to care for that tree. An immature gardener would be someone who got excited and planted a new tree and then when it bore fruit, went on to plant another, forgetting the first. Each time running ahead for a new goal, and each time leaving the tree behind him to waste.

Letting It Die

Now sometimes things do happen and a tree is lost. I remember planting a rose garden once. Those rose bushes grew rapidly and before long they had yielded a whole crop of beautiful roses.

However, as winter came the roses died and the tree withered and turned brown. What happened to my beautiful roses? Instead of getting discouraged I pruned those dead looking trees and left them to rest for the winter.

When spring came I was astonished as I looked out of my window one day to see how those dead bushes had suddenly sprung to life and had produced a whole new crop of blossoms! What looked dead and dormant one day was vibrant with life the next.

It is not easy to see something that you poured so much time and effort into die in your hands. Perhaps you founded a church or a ministry and now it is withering before your eyes. Now is not the time to be discouraged.

Just like the gardener who prunes the tree and leaves it to rest for winter, you also need to cut away anything that is standing in the way of your calling and lay that ministry to the earth! Let it die, because even though it looks dead, it is being transformed and being made ready to resurrect when spring comes.

Same Spirit, Different Tree

If I was confused that the Lord told me to give up the work I started, I was even more confused when the prophetic gifts in me began to wane.

Just like those rose bushes, I watched how from one moment my prophetic ministry was in full blossom to suddenly withering and turning brown. At first I panicked, because I felt that I had missed God entirely.

Fortunately this was not the case. The reason for this was that time that the Lord wanted to lead me into the teaching ministry. Where I literally lived in the realm of the spirit before, I suddenly felt myself crashing to the ground into the reality of the Word and the meat of God's instruction for us through scripture.

My revelation now came from scripture and now, instead of counseling others through revelation, I would teach their problems away!

Just as the scripture says,

> *1 Corinthians 12:4 There are diversities of gifts, but the same Spirit.*
>
> *5 There are differences of ministries, but the same Lord.*
>
> *6 And there are diversities of activities, but it is the same God who works all in all.*

By Colette Toach

7 But the manifestation of the Spirit is given to each one for the profit of all.

I learned that I was operating with the same Holy Spirit, but that He was just manifesting himself through me in a different way now. It took me a while to understand fully what was happening inside and I must admit that it was a time of great death for me.

Before I always told my prophetic students, "Get out of your mind and learn to flow with the spirit." But the message that the Lord kept giving me now was, "Get out of the spirit and use your mind for once!"

It went against my very nature and I must confess that like Jacob of old, I struggled and fought with the Holy Spirit over this. I felt naked without that spiritual revelation. Just as naked I am sure a teacher would feel without his Strong's concordance!

However when I was willing to submit to the work God had for me and let that original tree go, a new ministry began to be birthed inside of me and that tender sapling, was the teaching ministry.

Now from teaching the prophets through example and by being there to show them what to do practically, the Lord led me to begin laying training out in a systematic, logical way.

I began teaching and writing, laying everything out in written form. I spent month's just receiving revelation from the Word and writing that revelation down, placing it into the new structure that God had given me.

I began to see a new tree beginning to grow. This tree was larger and encompassed more than just the prophetic ministry.

As I began to build a teaching structure, I produced a reproducing asset that was a hard copy and I began to reach way more people than I had before. I began to change more lives than I had before and I began to get the truths of the Word out to God's people!

Blending and Mending

In time the Lord began to combine what I had learned over the various phases. From my prophetic well drying up and my inkwell overflowing, I found a strange thing beginning to happen. A mixture began to take place in my ministry.

A combination of the prophetic and the teaching began to happen in my life. In planting my prophetic tree, I mentored and produced fruit in people's lives. In planting my teaching tree, I taught using the Word and produced fruit that could be spread and passed on to others, educating their minds and giving them a track to run on and on which to base their lives.

But the Lord is ever changing in His uniqueness! You can never get bored with following the Lord, for while His grace endures forever; His modus operandi has to be as trendsetting as anything you have known!

By Colette Toach

Just when I had settled into the teaching ministry and was well on my way to labeling myself as a teacher, He began to bring the prophetic revelation back that I had left nearly a full year before that.

Now he began to combine these two trees and I came to see that they stood next to one another in my apostolic garden. You see the Lord wanted me to mentor as well as set up a structure.

I needed both of these aspects for the mandate He had given me. Because of that not only could I raise up other trainers like myself, but I could give them a full training mechanism to use.

It reminds me of the work that Moses did. Not only did he raise up Joshua, but he left behind full instruction on what to do when they finally reached the Promised Land.

Consider Apostle Paul. You see the same trend in his life. It was not good enough just for him to pour everything he had into Timothy and Titus. He took it to a new level and left behind the structure for the New Testament church.

A structure that we still hold onto today.

The Big Picture

Now the same thing applies to you and your ministry. The Lord may be leading you out into ministry fields that you have not been in before. He may even be leading you to leave the ministry you founded for a short season, but never forget that the ministry you founded is a part of your garden and a part of the bigger picture.

Sometimes it is difficult to see the whole picture, but if you will be diligent in going where the Lord tells you to go and building what the Lord tells you to build, then you will find yourself doing a full circle and standing in the same spot in your garden that you began in maybe years before.

It is then that you will be able to look at your garden with a new perspective and see everything that the Lord had in mind.

It could be that you are being called to death right now. It could be that your first church disbanded or that your first ministry failed. In fact, if you are in apostolic training, it is very likely that you have a few failed ministries behind you. Imagine how Apostle Paul must have felt when he had that falling out with Barnabas.

I could imagine that he saw himself just doing what they always did together. But the Lord had bigger plans for Paul. Paul had a foundation to lay for the Church that Barnabas did not. Not until he was willing to let go of what he had before, could he establish the mandate God had given him.

The fruit of the ministries you have left behind continue to live in the hearts of those that the Lord brought to you at that time and they continue to live in you!

Just like my prophetic ministry never left me, in the same way those seeds that were sown in your heart and spirit during that time, will never leave you.

They will come to find their place at the end of your apostolic training to reflect a well-placed tree in a garden that is flourishing under the hand of the Lord!

Growing Up...
Transition from
Apostolic Child to Adult

Chapter 14– Growing Up... Transition From Apostolic Child to Adult

I distinctly remember what it was like to leave school. When you have passed through adolescence and on to adulthood, you think that you know what life is really like.

You can imagine how successful you will be one day and how you will run your own life just like you want to.

But as I am sure you also came to realize after leaving school and starting on your own, that it is not as easy as you first thought. You suddenly come to experience this thing called 'responsibility' and where you could let things go before, you could not do that anymore.

You did not have anyone there showing you what to do or an excuse to get away with things because you were too young to do them yet.

You had to learn to fend for yourself now and those fantastic ideas you had before leaving home flew smartly out of the window within the first month of heading out on your own.

After that something interesting begins to happen, as you find your way in this phase of life. You come to realize over time, that you no longer think like you did when you were in school, and even worse, you catch yourself saying things and doing things just like you learned from your teachers!

There comes a time in the life of a budding apostle, when he is called of God to step out of his womb and comfort zone and to step out into the unknown. Perhaps you were the assistant pastor of your church, perhaps you were a member or maybe you helped someone else establish their ministry.

All along, you are saying in your heart, "I would do things so differently! When the Lord releases me into my own ministry, I am going to set up my own rules and establish my own pattern."

However you will come to realize as you make that step out of your comfort zone, just like you left school, that things do not always go as you anticipated. You come to learn that there is a heavy responsibility in stepping out and doing things on your own.

However just as a child has to step out and make a life for themselves, you have to take this step before your training can begin.

Stepping out, Tripping up

I am sure that not all of the choices that you have made in life were the right ones. And so it is very important to test your heart when you finally do make that step to move out on your own.

You need to know that it is the Lord that is leading you and that you are not being driven by your own ambition or bitterness. Moses started out doing things in the wrong spirit. He looked at the Israelites affliction and tried to take matters in his own hands.

He stepped out to try and save them at the wrong time. Their hearts were not ready to receive him yet and the result of that wrong move led him to spend 40 years in the wilderness!

There is such a temptation to look at the leadership and to see all the wrongs. If you are an apostle, it is very likely that you see the wrongs before you see the rights!

You notice the flaws and the mistakes the leader makes and it burns in you to rectify them. Many times I am sure that you tried to bring change and received a cold reception and rejection. In all these things though you need to realize that the Holy Spirit is training you.

The Courts of Saul

There needs to be a season where you are in the "Courts of Saul". You need to remain there until God's given time. I remember living this lesson myself. I had been reared under the apostleship of my natural father.

I always had ideas and wanted to change things. And like any other arrogant apostle in training, I also thought my ideas were better and that I could do it better.

And then the Lord gave him the word to hand everything over to me for a season. This was my chance! I was placed at the helm of the ministry battleship and I could ride the waves any way I pleased.

Well the first day went alright, the second day I discovered that the waters on which the ministry ship traveled were rather turbulent and by the end of the week I thought I had shipwrecked it for sure! I came to realize that it took more than just having ideas and a vision to handle a large ministry!

It takes the timing of the Lord, the empowerment of His spirit and a team to back you and stand by your side. You see, your vision and your zeal for ministry is only going to take you so far.

What you need is training and experience and the only way that you are going to gain those things are going to be by following through every phase of training that the Holy Spirit takes you through.

Learning the Lessons

And so if you find yourself in a local church or under a ministry organization, what are your motivations for stepping out? Are you angry? Are you trying to prove something? Or have you received a direct word from God?

Because until you have finished learning every single lesson that you need to learn in that ministry, you are not ready to step out yet. Do you want to be like Moses and spend 40 years in the wilderness? It is up to you, but the Lord will take you through the same phase time and time again until you have learned all the lessons that you need to learn.

When you were a child, you were in no way ready to go and make it on your own. There were naturalistic skills that you needed to learn first.

Now you might find yourself leaving a church only to be led to another. Are you wondering what is happening to you? Could it not be that there are a few more things that God wants you to do?

Could it be that you have not finished learning yet? Do not be so keen to head out and try to make it on your own.

How Will You Know When It is Really Time to Leave?

You will know that it is time to leave, when you do not want to leave any longer!

Making It alone

The time does come when you are called of God to make that step and usually the call comes when you least expect it or want it. When you have finally found a place where you are comfortable, accepted and are doing well, that God will say, "It is time to be set apart for the work" just as Paul and Barnabas were set apart and sent out by the elders by the laying on of hands.

I remember when one my friends graduated and then left home for the first time. I do not think that he fully grasped what it meant to really go and make a life for himself. Every weekend he would still bring his laundry home for his mother to do and she would still do all his shopping for him.

Then he could not understand why his parents continued to tell him what to do with his life! He used to get so frustrated! He would say to me, "I have left home, but my parents are still telling me what to do with my life and how to run it."

Well you could not blame his parents could you? He had not really moved out, he just lived in a different place, but still hung on to the benefits of being a child in that home.

Now when the Lord leads you to head out on your own and to establish the work that He has given you, there will be that same tendency in you. There will be that tendency, to leave your place of comfort, but to hold on 'just in case.'

But you see, until you are willing to let go entirely and take full responsibility for your calling, you will not be ready for all that the Lord has for you. You will be as my friend, who is trying to do his own thing and then getting upset because his parents were interfering!

You cannot have both; you can have one or the other. Either you will retain your position in your church, organization or denomination, or you will head out on your own and take with you the things that you learned.

So if the Lord has been trying to bring you to a place of burning your bridges and of leaving everything behind, then you are right on track with your apostolic training. I think that all of us wish it could be different.

Wouldn't it just be easier if we continued to let Mom do our laundry, while we went and chased after those dreams of success? But it is not like that in the natural world and it is not like that in the spirit either.

If you look at the life of David, you will see how he had to make that choice. You will see how he had finally been accepted into the house of Saul and had got settled. There were many things that he learned here and I am sure that he figured that it was here that he would see the throne just like God promised!

Doesn't that sound so perfect? It is easy to see how the Lord is going to raise you up as an apostle and as a leader when you are functioning as a leader in the ministry of another or under the apostleship of another.

But it is not so easy to see yourself as that leader when you have to leave just like David had to leave the courts of Saul.

Soon David found himself in the Cave of Adullam and yet it was here in the wilderness that his true kingship began to show and just three years from being banished to the wilderness, did the Lord raise him up and set him on the throne of Judah. And so as the Lord calls you to leave everything behind, your associations, your positions and your titles, you are likely to find yourself in the wilderness very much like David did.

But you cannot hold on to both. You cannot stay at home and leave. If the Lord is asking you to step out, then step out you must. You must be as Elisha who burned his oxen and his cart, making a declaration that he will never return.

Do you have that kind of conviction in what God has called you to do? Are you willing to put your money where your mouth is, so to speak? Not out of rebellion, not out of jealousy, but simply out of direct obedience to God?

Taking It All With You

There is something very special about taking that ultimate step and I hope that you will learn from the mistakes of our heroes of faith. Do not be like Moses who ran ahead too soon and do not be like David who hung on until the last minute.

Step out in the right timing and be sensitive to the voice of God through your own relationship with the Lord and through the confirmation of your spouse and others the Lord will bring your way.

But do not be discouraged as you step out, because everything that you have faced and encountered is part of your training. Every lesson that you learned, you get to take with you.

You will take with you all the principles and teaching that you received during these times. Then you will take them and the Lord will add to them and you will establish something new that is unmistakably yours.

Moses

You see Moses learned all he needed to about the Egyptians and the courts of Pharaoh. He knew how to approach Pharaoh and how to get an audience with him. He knew the protocol.

Had he not known any of these things, it is unlikely that he would have even had made it to Pharaoh's front door! In fact Josephus even says that according to history, Moses had instruction in battle.

It is no wonder he could teach the children of Israel how to handle themselves in war.

By the time he had led the Israelites out of Egypt, he had learned many lessons and then applied those lessons in bringing them back to the mountain of God! Not only could he lead them, but he could also train them to defend themselves and take the Promised Land.

By Colette Toach

The same applies to you and while you will continue going through many changes, you will use those things you learned and all of those lessons will suddenly make sense when the Lord finally releases you!

David

David also had a great advantage from learning from Saul. Saul was his mentor and perhaps even a spiritual father of sorts. David learned many things about being a king and ruling a people in the courts of Saul.

He learned much from Jonathan also and when David took the throne he could apply these principles to his own kingship. The Lord could set David on the throne quickly, because David had learned about kingship under Saul.

So realize that just as you leave home and take all those naturalistic principles with you, so also will you be taking all you have learned from your spiritual homes with you into your new mandate.

You may be leaving home, but you are carrying in your heart the foundation that was laid there by the mighty men and women of God that the Lord sent to shape and impart to you. We will be looking in the next chapter at apostolic mentoring and fathering and perhaps by the end of that, you will be able to easily identify your mentors and spiritual parents.

You will also learn that just as you threw some of the things that your folks did in their home out of the widow and established your own code of living, that as an apostle, you will do the same. So continue to wait on the Lord and to keep your heart humble before Him.

Ask Him what step He wants you to take right now and then take it in faith, take it in humility and take it knowing that His hand covers you every step of the way!

Mentoring Versus Apostolic Fathering

Chapter 15 – Mentoring Versus Apostolic Fathering

1 Corinthians 4:14 I do not write these things to shame you, but as my beloved children I warn you.

15 For though you might have ten thousand instructors in Christ, yet you do not have many fathers; for in Christ Jesus I have begotten you through the gospel.

16 Therefore I urge you, imitate me.

17 For this reason I have sent Timothy to you, who is my beloved and faithful son in the Lord, who will remind you of my ways in Christ, as I teach everywhere in every church.

18 Now some are puffed up, as though I were not coming to you.

19 But I will come to you shortly, if the Lord wills, and I will know, not the word of those who are puffed up, but the power.

20 For the kingdom of God is not in word but in power.

21 What do you want? Shall I come to you with a rod, or in love and a spirit of gentleness?

Having grown up in a home where my father was the mast of our family ship, so to speak, it is hard for me to imagine a life without having had a father. Could you imagine growing up without the guidance and direction of a father?

Perhaps you had a bad relationship with your father, or maybe your father left home when you were young. No matter who you are and where you come from, there is always this space in your heart for a father.

Whether you found that space met in your natural father or not, it exists nonetheless and as you enter the arena of ministry, it is this natural need that will cause you to look around and seek out someone who would instruct and guide you in your calling.

Now this is a vital process of your growth and in this chapter we are going to look at what the difference is between a mentor and a spiritual father, how you can identify your spiritual father, and finally your responsibility to your spiritual father.

A Note About Apostolic Versus Spiritual Parenting

Before I delve into this subject I want to clarify that I am speaking here of spiritual parenting at an Apostolic Level. I am sure that even through your life you have had many who have served as spiritual fathers and mothers to you.

Regular Spiritual Parenting

Those who took you through a natural reparenting process or even taught you everything you needed to know about the Lord. They may have even been the ones who brought you to the Lord and fed you the milk you needed to grow up.

This process of spiritual parenting is a natural event as we receive from others in our Christian walk. I am sure that even now as you look back you can pick out those that had a special place in your heart and life.

These leaders were more than just spiritual leaders to you. They also had a powerful impact on your natural life. Often being a surrogate to replace your own natural parents. As the Lord has used Craig and I, we have often fulfilled this role in others.

To these folks we are not just spiritual leaders, but natural surrogate parents, to help them displace the negative influences and experiences that their natural parents put into them. Then imparting to each what they needed to rise up in their calling and in their lives and even their careers!

We have even parented those whose vision and calling were completely different to ours! To them we are natural and spiritual parents and some even lovingly refer to us as "Mom and Dad".

It is in this relationship where both the mother and father are needed and here you will see women rise up as mother surrogates as well as men who rise up as father surrogates.

By Colette Toach

If you had to look in the Word, I think one of the best examples of this is the relationship that Samuel had with Eli. Another good example of spiritual motherhood is the relationship between Naomi and Ruth.

In Eli's case, he was not only Samuel's spiritual covering, but became a natural father to him also. However, you will notice that Samuel followed a call completely different to Eli and received a separate mandate all together.

Apostolic Fatherhood

Now when it comes to Apostolic Parenting the rules change quite a bit. This relationship goes beyond being a natural surrogate to a point where you receive the actual mandate of your apostolic father.

To be able to receive this mandate, you need to also be an apostle just as Timothy and Silas were. So from here onwards I am speaking of the Apostolic level of parenting. It is the kind of relationship where you receive surrogate parenting, as well as the actual mandate that your spiritual father has.

The Difference Between Mentor and Father

When I was in school I was terribly insecure. Standing up in front of the class to deliver a speech for my final English mark in the final year of school was a nightmare. I did not know what to do.

I did relatively well in English class and I did not lack for ideas, but my confidence was really lacking. Not knowing what to do I sought out my English teacher to perhaps give me direction on what to do and how to overcome this problem.

And so I poured out my heart and she gave me direction and some advice to follow. She told me how to take a breath at each period point. She taught me how I needed to try and keep eye contact with my audience as much as possible, only glancing at my notes for a second or two to find my place.

But the more I developed a relationship with this teacher, I came to realize that she could only help me so much and that she could not really fill the need that I had for overcoming this insecurity.

She gave me some great principles to apply but I needed more than just principles, I needed a code of ethics. I needed to change the way I looked at life.

After bumping my head a few times, I came to realize that the only person who could give me the kind of direction I was looking for was my father. And so I finally decided to suck in my pride and turn to him for help. In a very short time, he had shown me what to do and how to present myself to the class.

He shared a principle with me that I will never forget. He said to me, "Colette, never forget that you are somebody special, because you have the King of Kings in you. Every time you meet a person or you stand to give a speech, do not stop to think what they are thinking of you, but rather ask yourself what you can do to help them.

When you meet a person or when you stand up in front of a crowd, think to yourself, 'Do you know that you are blessed today? Do you know that I have the answer to your need and that you are blessed just to have met me today?'"

He said that just by taking my eyes off myself and turning them towards the needs of others, knowing that I had an answer through the wisdom of Christ that I would never need to fear insecurity again.

Just this one principle turned my life around and when I grew up and took my turn to stand behind the pulpit, this principle was burned so strongly in me that I did not falter for a minute.

Now the principles that my teacher taught me were great. In fact, I use them all of the time, but they did not give me direction for my life and they did not help me overcome those deep rooted insecurities that I was struggling with.

The Mentor

Now if you look at the pictures I have given here, you will understand very easily the difference between a Mentor and a Apostolic Father. Or as Paul states *in 1 Corinthians 4:15, Instructors and Fathers.*

You will have many mentors in your life and you will learn from them all. And so just like my teacher gave me some great principles to use for presenting my speech, so will the Lord bring mentors to you for a season at a time so that they might impart their knowledge and experience to you.

You might have your first mentor at salvation, who will teach you all that you needed to know about being a Christian. You might have had a pastor who then mentored you in the Word and Christian living.

A little later you might have had an evangelist mentoring you in how to win the lost. In fact you might have thousands of instructors, just as Paul said. Yet you only have one father.

You see, when I left school, I left all of my teachers behind. Sure enough, I took all their knowledge with me, but I left their class and that level of my life behind. And so it is very important to realize that a mentorship relationship is temporary.

In the previous chapter I spoke of how the Lord would take you from church to church to teach you some things. Well each of these seasons in your life mentored you. Perhaps you were mentored by the pastor, maybe you simply received instruction from a church member or from the teaching given at that church.

Outgrowing the Mentor

In my illustration, even though I gained a lot of knowledge from my teachers, I could not stay in school forever. There had to come a time when I had to leave and apply those principles. But the time did come when I returned one day for a visit. And do you know what I discovered?

I found out that my teachers were not really as clever as I thought they were. In fact, I was quite confused. In my mind, I had seen them so above me, but as I returned I saw that I had learned far beyond what they knew in my own realm.

What happened? As I moved on and began to receive instruction from other sources, I outgrew my old teachers. I went into areas that they were not familiar with and so you can already see why the break with the mentor must come.

For you to rise up and be all that the Lord has for you, you need to receive all you can from your mentor and then move on if you wish to outgrow them. You cannot outgrow them while they continue to give you instruction.

And so the Lord will lead you time and time again to break from your mentor. Not because the mentorship is a bad thing, but rather because it is time for the spiritual adolescent in you to move on and grow up beyond that phase.

And so with each thing that the Lord wants to teach you, He will bring you a mentor to teach you what you need to know. You will have many different teachers, in many different forms. You might receive your instruction from books, maybe from a leader in the church, a best friend or even from a co-worker.

So look back on your life and identify those that mentored you in natural things and in spiritual things. Can you pick them out? Can you see how instrumental they were in making you the person that you are today?

Duration of Mentorship

In my personal experience, I have come to expect a mentorship relationship at an apostolic level to last about 9 months to be complete. It seems that this is about the amount of time that the Lord needs to do all that He desires in a student.

I also noted that not every single person that the Lord sent me came to receive the same thing. The Lord sent some to gain understanding sometimes on just one aspect of my ministry and life.

There were some that I imparted all of my knowledge and gifts relating to the prophetic ministry. Then there were others who just came to glean an understanding of how to enter into a relationship with the Lord. Still others were sent to me so that I might teach them how to become a leader.

In each case, the Lord wanted me to mentor them in something very specific. Not many of my disciples received all that I had, because each had a different need and the Lord only needed me to meet one of them for that season.

Some returned for additional phases of mentoring for different things. But in each case I noted a period of about 9 months that the Lord had us together. (Note that we are speaking here of fivefold ministry mentorship. Mentorship at a lower level relating to natural things, salvation and normal Christian living can take different amounts of time depending on the disciple.)

Breaking Links

When the Lord had completed the work for that season in that person, He brought a sword of division, so that they might move on and also release me to pour into another person. This division sometimes came through conflict, at times the Lord would just give me the word and I would sever it and break the links. Each time was unique and the Lord had His hand in them all.

So if there are any mentors that you have been hanging on to, then you must know that it is time to let them go. Until you let go of them, you cannot move on and learn the next thing that the Lord wants you to learn.

If you go back to that mental list that you made of all your mentors, it would do you good to sit down after reading this and to break links with each mentor.

When in personal ministry with students, I have had to lead them through breaking spiritual links with past mentors, because even though they have moved on in life, they are still holding on in their hearts and remain tied to that mentor.

So let me make it very clear, when a mentorship relationship is over ...it is over! When Elijah left on a chariot, Elisha could not go with him. He was left behind to complete his own mandate.

So make a resolution right now to move on. Then as you identify all of your mentors and let them go, I will lead you on to understanding spiritual fatherhood.

Apostolic Fatherhood

When I was an adolescent I would delight in knowing something that my father did not know. It was a challenge, but every now and then I managed to do it. I took great pleasure in being able to teach him something.

Twenty something years down the line and I still found myself trying to learn something that my father did not know. I do not know about your father, but mine just seemed to know everything about everything.

As I grew up and discovered most of what there was to know about life, I found out that my father had already found that out before me. When I had kids and learned about being a parent, I discovered that my father had known about all of that before me as well.

No matter where I stepped in life, it seemed that he had been there before me. And so it should be. My father had been before me. He had been where I was going and had already lived what I was living.

Two Steps Ahead

I soon came to discover that this also applied in the spiritual realm. No matter how much I grew in the Word or learned about the spiritual life, I came to discover that my father had been that way before me!

Now that is what an apostolic father looks like. You do not outgrow an apostolic father easily in the same way that you outgrow a mentor. Why is this? Well the main reason is that an apostolic father never stops growing!

He is always one step ahead, living everything before you, so that when you get to that stage in the road, he has already left his mark on the signpost! You can run hard or try to push ahead, but you will always find that he has gone that way before you!

And so you are beginning to see one of the major differences between a mentor and a spiritual father. You will outgrow a mentor, but you will not outgrow your spiritual father!

He will always remain senior to you and just as my natural father will remain a step ahead of me in years and in living, so will your spiritual father, if he sticks on the heels of the Father, remain ahead of you in experience and understanding.

Taking It All

The next thing I came to understand as I grew up is that teachers came and went, but my father remained. I would be with a teacher who would teach me one subject, but my father taught me on many different subjects.

A mentor will instruct you in one area and it will likely be the one thing that they are strong at. And so as I would have an English teacher, a math teacher and a biology teacher, each would instruct me in their expertise. But when it came to my Dad, I did not just learn one thing from him. I learned from all the realms of his knowledge.

You see this very much in the life of Paul. Paul instructed many and if you read his letters to his churches, you will see how he instructed some in the way of dealing with the flesh, some he instructed on how the church should be run and others he gave correction.

Timothy, however who was his spiritual son, received everything that he had. In fact, he says as much in: *1 Corinthians 4:17 For this reason I have sent Timothy to you, who is my beloved and faithful son in the Lord,*

who will remind you of my ways in Christ, as I teach
everywhere in every church.

Timothy knew everything that Paul taught to the
degree that he could go out and preach it himself. This
is how you can identify someone who is your spiritual
father.

He is someone that you received everything from. You
do not just receive his teachings or his instruction or
his guidance or an impartation of anointing and gifts,
you receive them all!

Relationship Permanent

As I left school, my teachers remained behind, but as I
left home, my father was always there to go back to.
We got together on Christmas and birthdays and if I
needed direction and guidance about my life, I could
go and glean some of his wisdom.

This perfectly describes the relationship between a
spiritual son and father.

He might not always be there to tell you what to do or
where to go, but he remains there for counsel when
you need it and a shelter to run to when you need it.
You will always have the same spiritual blood running
through your veins that will tie you together no matter
how many oceans divide you.

This is why God is raising up apostolic fathers in our
church generation, because you need that shelter and

that guidance. It is not good enough just having the "know-how" and understanding of how things work, but you need someone that is willing to give you their knowledge, experience, principles and most importantly their hearts.

Once again I think that Paul says it the best, He says:

> *2 Timothy 1:2 To Timothy, a beloved son: Grace, mercy, and peace from God the Father and Christ Jesus our Lord.*
>
> *3 I thank God, whom I serve with a pure conscience, as my forefathers did, as without ceasing I remember you in my prayers night and day;*

Timothy was on Paul's mind 24 hours a day! Who has you in their thoughts night and day? The apostolic father is one who carries his children in his heart and looks out for their future.

Giving Direction

If we go back to my first illustration and the principles that my father gave me to live by, you will see another principle that identifies the mentor as being different from a spiritual father. My teacher gave me principles and teaching, but my father gave me something to live by, he gave me direction for my life.

An apostolic father is someone who will give you direction and help you find your mandate. He will show you which way you need to be going. He will take everything that you have learned and all the principles that you gained from all of your teachers and he will put it into a full picture of where you are and where you are headed.

Are you looking for your mandate? Are you looking for the full picture of your ministry? Could it be that you need to be asking the Lord who your spiritual father is?

Paul instructed Timothy continually and even imparted gifts to him. He told him how to run his church and what the Lord was expecting of him. He gave Timothy the direction that he needed to fulfill the calling that burned in him.

The Price

It is sometimes a heavy price to admit that you need to look into the eyes of another. It is like the child who left home and discovered that maybe his parents did know a thing or two after all!

Only when you can come to the place of submission and willingness to put your own agendas aside will you be ready for your spiritual father to give you direction.

If you do not know who your spiritual father is, then you need to be seeking the Lord as to whether He has one for you and who he is. If you already have a spiritual father, then you need to decide if you have everything that your spiritual father has.

Do you flow in all of his anointing and gifts? Do you think like him yet? Can you stand up and preach all of his sermons like Timothy could quote Paul?

Because until you are able to say yes to all of those questions, then you need to remain submitted as a child in the home of their parent and to obey, receive and grow in the environment that the Lord has given you.

The time will come soon enough when you will leave home and blaze a trail of your own under his direction and guidance, but for now it is time to admit your spiritual childishness and to receive from the one that the Lord has placed in your life.

Being a Good Spiritual Son or Daughter

Chapter 16 – Being a Good Spiritual Son or Daughter

There is a subject that I have mentioned briefly in this book so far and it is the subject of servanthood. Along the road of apostolic training I learned that the greatest lesson I could ever receive on leadership was to first learn to be a true servant.

Perhaps you are familiar with this little story:

Little Johnny was standing up in the back of the classroom. His teacher looked at him and said, "Johnny sit down!" but he did not want to sit down, but kept on standing.

His teacher told him again, "Johnny, sit down!" Still Johnny remained standing. After some time of giving threats and telling Johnny to obey, Johnny finally took his seat. On the outside, it looked as if Johnny had obeyed and submitted to his teacher, but on the inside, Johnny was still standing up!

It is not good enough to submit because you have to or even because it is the right thing to do. The lesson the Lord wants you to learn is to submit out of true humility and love. This is one of the main reasons why apostolic fatherhood and sonship is based on a relationship of love.

I remember a time at the very beginning of our ministry when we were having a meeting with perspective students to assess their readiness for training.

One of the questions that they asked was, "We do not feel comfortable with being told what to do. We have been under dominating leaders before that only used us to extend their own vision and so we do not want to end up with the same thing here!"

It was not easy for us to explain at that time, the concept of submission that we had learned. It was not an enforced one, but one based on relationship. In this relationship we all had to learn our place and one of those places was to submit! First as spiritual son and daughter and then as spiritual parents ourselves.

There is no getting around it and if you truly want to rise up into all that God has for you, then you must learn to submit and to be a true leader. It is easy enough to say that you trust the Holy Spirit to guide you and give you direction, but are you willing to trust the Holy Spirit in someone else?

If you want a spiritual father, then it comes with a price. It will require that you submit and that you learn and that you are willing to be molded after that person, taking on their mandate and vision as your own.

Catching the Vision

For many, this price is too big to pay. I cannot tell you how many apostles in preparation have come to us asking for direction and parenting. However, when we laid out the price, they suddenly do not want it anymore!

They want to come and receive of you and take all that you have and then go their own way and build up their own name. It would be like a son being born into a family, eating the food off their table, receiving their love, care and education and then leaving, changing his name and not wanting anything to do with them. Saying to himself, "I will start a new family as if I was not born into that other family!"

In the natural we would not respect that son very much, would we? It would be like Jesus coming to earth and saying, "The Father sent me, but now that I am here I will do it my own way and do what I think is better. I do not see why I have to die on the cross, I will find another way of doing it!"

Did the disciples say after Jesus left, "Well the Lord has given everything into our hands now, we will change things? We do not see why we need to change the way we live, we should continue under the law and just adapt some of the new principles He taught us and make a whole new pattern!"

Can you even imagine what a state the Church would be in if they did that? No, if you have a spiritual father then their vision and mandate will become your own. When you are ready for that, you will discover that the Lord planted the same spiritual DNA in both of you

By Colette Toach

anyway, so in essence his vision simply enhances yours!

Joshua did not alter the pattern that Moses gave him, but it says in scripture that: *Joshua 11:23 So Joshua took the whole land, according to all that the Lord had said to Moses; and Joshua gave it as an inheritance to Israel according to their divisions by their tribes. Then the land rested from war.*

Joshua did everything according to what Moses had laid out. He not only received instruction and the anointing from Moses, He received his vision and mandate also.

So what if you do not have the same vision or desire as your spiritual father? Then it is up to you to lay aside your own visions and to make a choice. I have already taken you through the process of death of a vision so you should understand by now what I am talking about.

If you received those visions prior to having a spiritual father, then you should be laying them down even more so. It is only once you do that, that you will find your true vision. God put you here for a reason! Do you think he would have you take on a vision that He did not intend for you to fulfill?

The first step is to make a choice to receive. And then the next step is to remain close to your spiritual father to receive everything that he has. As you open your heart to receive, you will catch his vision and the anointing to fulfill it!

You will begin to see things like he does and you will begin to share his same zeal. Before you even know it, you will burn with the same fire. You cannot help but receive.

If you are like little Johnny and just submitting on the outside because you have to, you will not really experience change in your heart. There is a great price to pay being a spiritual parent and a spiritual son and it is up to you to decide if you want to pay it.

Our team is so diverse in their desires and passions for God. Yet somehow the visions that were buried under all their pre-conceived ideas were a perfect match for ours as the leaders. We were of the same tribe and as they came in line, all our pieces could be brought together to make a whole.

It is only when you take this step, that the apostle can put everyone in place correctly. A time is coming when you will be the one requiring others to submit to you – before you qualify for that – are you ready to submit to others?

The Benefits

So now that you know what will be required of you as a spiritual son, what are the benefits of such a relationship? I will share here from the Word and from personal experience so that you can get the full picture for yourself.

Try to identify as you read along here those that the Lord put into your life that you felt where spiritual fathers. Did you treat them correctly? Did you submit and receive from them as you were supposed to? Only you will know what was truly in your heart.

1. Receiving the Fruits

The first benefit of receiving from a spiritual father is that you get to receive the fruits of their labor just like Timothy received from Paul. I have faced many years of preparation and training and it is why those that I mentor can rise up quickly. They do not need to face everything I did!

Because Craig and I had faced those deaths and those trials, others are able to step right in and to receive and learn from us without having to face the same mistakes themselves.

We train our team and spiritual children how to minister, flow in the anointing and what the correct pattern for the church is. If they had to try and learn all of that themselves, it would take them the same number of years it has taken us. Instead they are given the privilege of receiving everything at a very young age and rising up to a level that would usually take years to accomplish.

2. The Protection and Love

The greatest benefit, is the protection and love that an apostolic father gives. It is not easy to step out into the unknown and take the land. It is always encouraging to know that someone has planned the way and can give you direction.

I remember the first time that the Lord released our first spiritual children to step out on their own. It was a call that took them across the ocean and it was no small task! A new country and a new work... were they ready?

Not a day went by when they were not in touch to get support and direction. Above all, to simply hear our voices to encourage them to press through, no matter how difficult things were.

The best part about having a spiritual parent is not necessarily always having all the answers at your fingertips, but that you do not need to face the unknown alone! It was a completely new experience for us to be on the "other side" this time.

We remembered well what it felt like to be thrust into the unknown and to start a new work in a new country. We knew the struggles with the language, change of food and terminology. We could not walk the road for them, but we could sure help them spot the potholes we fell into!

By Colette Toach

You will come to learn as you walk the apostolic road of training, that it becomes more and more lonely the more you press on. There are less that understand you and as friends and family fall away, your spiritual father will always be there to cover and protect you.

He is already two steps ahead of you and if you need help or have any questions, he is there with the answer.

He is there to cover your mistakes and just as I taught you about apostolic leadership, the apostolic father is the ultimate leader! He not only watches over you, but takes responsibility for your mistakes.

There have been many times when one of our team made a mistake. Perhaps in the natural they would deserve to take on all the consequences of that mistake, but we have been where they are now. We have made the same mistakes and while we will certainly have a good talk about it, we are there to cover them. We are there to take responsibility. God told us to put them in that position – their mistakes are our mistakes.

So once the dust settles, we take them aside and bring correction and instruction, so that it does not happen again.

There is no price too great for this kind of relationship. And as you look at this picture with me I pray that you are seeing very clearly that the apostolic fatherhood relationship is not one of autocratic domination, but a relationship of love and understanding.

It is not about someone being the "head apostle" and you having to submit. But rather of him being the spiritual father and you submitting out of love and respect.

Is this not how Timothy and Titus submitted to Paul? Is this not how Peter submitted to Jesus? Did Peter submit to Jesus because he had to?

No, he submitted because he found in Jesus what he was looking for. And in the end it was his love for the Lord that drew him even closer. What a lovely passage this is: *John 21:15 So when they had eaten breakfast, Jesus said to Simon Peter, "Simon, son of Jonah, do you love Me more than these?" He said to Him, "Yes, Lord; You know that I love You." He said to him, " Feed My lamb."*

Peter loved Jesus with all of his life and this is what qualified him to receive the mandate directly from the hand of Jesus. It was not his skill or his great show of submission, but his love.

It is this love for your spiritual father that will redeem you time and time again even when you fail. And even if your spiritual father makes a mistake, then it is this love that brings the hand of the Holy Spirit upon him to give him the answers he needs to give you.

By Colette Toach

3. The Direction

It is easy to look within and see what burns in your heart. However, it is not so easy to take all of that and do something with it! Right now you are very much like a wild stallion that has all this power and ability, but is running wild in the fields and accomplishing nothing!

The apostolic father would take you, put a harness on you, join you to a team of horses and cause you to accomplish something!

Together you will accomplish a task greater than any one person could do. But again this comes with a price.

It means putting down your own agendas and from doing the things that you wanted to do and receiving the vision and direction from the Lord through your apostolic father. Is this not what Titus and Timothy did under Paul?

Is this not what the disciples did under Jesus? Matthew the tax collector gave up his job, Peter, James and John gave up their fishing business and Paul gave up his great education. Everyone gave up their own vision and submitted to the vision of the Lord to accomplish a single purpose.

And just look at what they accomplished! They turned the world upside down. The word says so! *Acts 17:6 But when they did not find them, they dragged Jason and some brethren to the rulers of the city, crying out,*

"These who have turned the world upside down have come here too."

If only that could be said of the Church today! This will only be accomplished as you take your place as a spiritual son or as a spiritual father. Together you will accomplish so much. Is this not after all the pattern that Jesus set up in His original church? Should we not be following after this pattern again?

So submit yourself to receive direction. As your spiritual father is led of the Lord, he will take what is within you and give you the direction that you need.

Sure enough, there will be times you will be tested or asked to do things that perhaps you do not want to do at first, but in every case, it will cause you to grow and to accomplish what the Lord had put into you all along.

It was not a case of fulfilling the vision that God had given your apostolic father. But rather it became a case of finding our place in the vision God has given your apostolic father.

Guidelines

I want to end this chapter with a few guidelines for you to make note of and to remember for future reference. As you begin to live the things that I have shared in this book, you will find that the things that I have shared will come back to you again and again.

Do not think that once you have finished reading that it is over for you! Not at all, you will read and understand just some of what I have shared so far. Then you will go away and live some more of it and then when you come back to read this again, you will understand a whole new dimension that you did not get before!

1. One Apostolic Father at a Time

It is not possible to have more than one apostolic father at a time. You cannot have this in the natural and so you cannot have it in the spiritual! Perhaps you did sit under the apostolic fatherhood of someone, but you ended up leaving.

Does this mean then that you cannot have another spiritual father? Not at all. It means though that you will need to let go of the old to take on the new.

You can only receive in this way from one person. Fatherhood is not like mentorship and you cannot decide that you will take one or two things from this spiritual father and then when you have had enough, change spiritual fathers!

This is a very different relationship to a mentoring one and you need to understand the implications of this when you decide to commit yourself to such an apostolic father. I thank the Lord that we were given the opportunity to grow under one spiritual father and to reach the potential in that relationship.

Once that relationship ended, we could look to God the Father directly as such a father and because we had learned to submit to and follow a man of God, we could apply those same lessons to following the Lord.

I know that we could never have achieved this closeness with the Father without learning to submit to a spiritual father first. Who else would care to give you the time and the love? Who else in this world cares more about your direction and calling than their own?

Only a spiritual father does and as we look at this subject a little more in the next chapter, you will come to realize that the price a spiritual father pays is greater than the price that you pay.

It is easy to receive and to have everything handed to you, but it is not as easy to go through death for others!

2. Changing Your Identity

I think that this is the most difficult part for any apostle. If you are called to be an apostle, you hold on tightly to what God has promised you. I was the same and always sought to be independent and do things my own way.

In my mind I could do things better than my leaders, using my own ideas! I can just see the spiritual adolescent in me back then!

It is like Peter who said to the Lord,

Matthew 16:22 Then Peter took Him aside and began to rebuke Him, saying, "Far be it from You, Lord; this shall not happen to You!"

23 But He turned and said to Peter, "Get behind Me, Satan! You are an offense to Me, for you are not mindful of the things of God, but the things of men."

He thought he knew better than the Lord. What was Jesus talking about? Peter thought he could do it better. We all know the humbling experiences he went through though, don't we? Only when he gave up everything and even his own identity did the Lord raise him up.

I was like the story I shared of little Johnny many times. I would sit down on the outside to make a good show of submission, but on the inside I was standing loudly and proudly, sure that I could do it differently.

Only when I learned to let go of my own independence and what I thought my part was, could the Lord release me to take my place. The most amazing thing was though, that when I finally let go of my identity, the Lord raised me up and I was given a place where I was unique!

It is not that the Lord does not want you to stand out. He just wants you to learn to truly submit first. If you have a spiritual father, realize that this vision is not just about you any longer.

It is about you, your apostolic father and his other spiritual sons and daughters also! Each one of you needs to find a place. As you are willing to let go of your own ideas and ideals, you will be put in a place where those original ideas and visions are given the liberty to be expressed that causes everyone to benefit from it.

3. The Spiritual Family

How could I even begin to explain the benefit of the spiritual family the Lord has given us? I look at Paul and Silas in prison and see how they sang hymns until the prison shook. I see how the disciples shared in their tribulations and in their successes together.

I can see them gathered in the upper room after the death of Jesus, consoling one another and wondering what to do next.

When you look at Jesus' disciples, you see that each came from such a different walk of life. In just three years, the Lord had made them into a family that remained together even after he had ascended.

When you are going through trials or are facing hard times, the most encouraging thing is to have a spiritual family that is there to encourage and motivate you.

4. Either You Are in or You Are Out

You need to come to a place of decision. Either you are going to submit yourself to a spiritual father or you are not. You cannot expect to gain the benefits and not pay the price.

You cannot sit on the outskirts and take the teachings and the anointing and then decide to do things your own way. You need to learn to be a team player and as you do this, you will see yourself accomplishing more than you ever thought you would.

We live in a world where everyone is going off on their own tangent. As unfortunate as it is, this is happening in the Church also and you see many who try to raise themselves up in the eyes of man and dominate control over others.

Perhaps you have been under a leader like this and you are afraid to commit yourself to that again. Perhaps you are that kind of leader and you do not want to give up your control.

Either way the Lord is raising up His End Times apostles and He is doing it His way. He is establishing His pattern and it is going to take change on your part for that pattern to become a reality.

You will need to lean on the Holy Spirit more than you ever have and truly come to trust in Him! You will need to learn to trust Him in others and trust Him to vindicate you when you feel that you have been wronged.

As you step forward and take your place as a spiritual son or daughter I pray that the Lord will direct your steps and cause you to be a part of the mighty move He is bringing to the Church and this world!

Raising Your Own Spiritual Sons and Daughters

Chapter 17 – Raising Your Own Spiritual Sons and Daughters

I had so many things to say about how my parents brought us up. One thing that I always complained about was being told to go to bed early! I always found a way out of having to get to bed on time. I would make excuses, complain and whine as much as I could before finally give in and go to bed.

As I grew up and had my own children I had to stifle a smile or two when I saw my own daughters doing the same with me. If you have children of your own, then perhaps you can identify. If they are not "needing the toilet" just minutes after lights out, they need a drink of water, are hungry or a common favorite in my home is, "Mommy I just want to ask you something quickly ..."

This can go on for at least an hour before they finally realize that I am not going to let them stay up. I can now relate to my own parents' frustrations. I have shared with you so far on how to be a good spiritual son or daughter, but let's take a brief look now at how you can learn to become a good spiritual parent yourself.

You will come to find that as you receive from your spiritual father, that the Lord will bring others to you so that you can pour into them also and so the pattern continues downward and everything you received you pour out to those the Lord brings you.

By Colette Toach

1. Your Fruit

The first thing you need to keep in mind is that an apostle's disciples will reflect his leadership and calling. A true apostle will raise disciples that reflect his image and stand firmly and go out and bear much fruit. The Scriptures say that we will be known by our fruit.

You will often hear, "Your fruit is the works you have established or the way you live your life."

However, this is not always true. We can always put on a good show. You can always be like little Johnny who sits down on the outside and stands up on the inside. So then how do you judge the fruit in a person? Is it the way that they live?

Have you ever had the opportunity to counsel a person who is struggling with something and said to them, "You have sin and bitterness in your life?" only for them to respond with, "Well show it to me in my fruit. I do well. I do good works. I am a good person?"

Well if I was going to judge a person by the works that they did, then I do not think that I would be a very good judge at all. Considering the fact that Jesus spent more time with harlots than with the Pharisees, we can assume right away that we cannot consider the outward appearance of a person as a sign of their spiritual fruit! Even unbelievers have good fruit if you want to look at it that way.

So what is your fruit then? Your disciples are your fruit. Your spiritual children are your fruit. That is what your fruit is.

So if you want to judge the work of an apostle then you would judge him by his spiritual children, because that is his fruit. If you want to really see what is in an apostle, have a word with his spiritual children and you will get to see what is really in him.

Would you be confident enough to have somebody come and question somebody who is under your leadership? Are you confident enough in what the Lord has put into you? Are you confident enough that you have poured correctly into those the Lord has sent you?

This will be a good place to start if you want to assess your success in ministry. If you have people that the Lord has sent you to receive from you, can you see yourself in their lives? Do you see them living as you do and teaching as you do? Are there things that you see in them that you do not like? Then perhaps you need to look at yourself first to see what you have poured into them.

2. Paying the Price

> *John 15:16 You did not choose Me, but I chose you and appointed you that you should go and bear fruit, and that your fruit should remain, that whatever you ask the Father in My name He may give you.*

17 These things I command you, that you love one another.

You will learn that you pay the price of death to the flesh, so that others can experience resurrection. You bring the seed to death in your own life so that they can walk in resurrection. You will face harder times than most. You will struggle to get an understanding of something, so that you can give the answers to others. This is a great price to pay because it means that nothing comes easy to you.

There are so many areas that the Lord has led me into that I would never have thought of myself. Natural and spiritual things. I guess with training being my primary mandate, I seemed to learn a little of everything.

Only as I started working with my own spiritual children did I see why I needed to learn these things. I could impart and teach each one the areas where they had a lack.

I made all the mistakes and took the long way around. Sometimes I even wandered in the desert around the mountain a couple of times. Why? So that when my time came to impart all I had to others, I could begin my instruction with ..."Do *not* do it that way!"

Sometimes the best instruction I have given has not been the road to take, but the roads to avoid. Of course you can only find these things out by walking down the wrong roads yourself. Certainly Apostle Paul could tell you a thing or two about that.

I look at our own lives and see the struggles that we faced in raising up the fivefold ministry in the Church. I see all the mistakes that we made and the many things that we tried before we started getting this right.

It is that road that qualifies us now to teach on these principles! If you want to instruct anyone on a subject, then you better have lived it yourself.

And so you will find yourself living many different things to help pour into those that the Lord gives you. Depending on the direction he has given your spiritual children will determine how much you will learn and live yourself.

You will face obstacles, trials and death to the flesh every step of the way. The Lord will purge you of everything that is "you" so that the spiritual DNA that you impart to others is 100% His and none of yours.

So do not think that you can hold onto all the things that you are so proud of. Just as your spiritual children will be called to give up everything to receive your mandate, God will require the same thing of you.

Much like Abraham who had to leave everything he was familiar with, the Lord will ask you to pay the same price. You cannot impart to others all the DNA and instruction you got from your own parents. Everything you have received before is colored with archetypes and mindsets.

By Colette Toach

No, to parent others, you need to be parented by the Lord yourself. Because of this, your learning will never end. You will receive more than one mandate and vision. Then as quickly as you receive them, you will pass them onto others.

Sometimes I think that I learn something for a single purpose: to pass it onto someone else who needed the anointing I have!

You will never be able to say as a spiritual father, "This is my vision." Because as the Lord brings you spiritual children, you will learn to accomplish many visions to be able to give them what they need to accomplish theirs.

3. Instruction and Discipline

Home schooling has become quite popular in this day and age and so you see parents taking on the responsibility of training and teaching their children, rather than leaving the job to a teacher.

An apostolic father fulfills a similar function for his spiritual children. No longer does he depend on others to teach and instruct those that the Lord has given him, but instead he takes the time to teach them himself. You will instruct them in the simplest matters to the most complex.

I found that as I started working with my spiritual children that the most profound effect I had on their lives was in the natural things.

From being there to instruct them how to teach or how to make a sale at work, I found that my job was very different to what I first anticipated.

You will be surprised to see how so much of our natural lives stand in the way of our calling. So often I find myself giving instruction on how to bring up children, handle a marital conflict or approach a boss correctly in the work place.

It is a full package when it comes to spiritual parenting. You are not a spiritual parent on Sundays and free the rest of the week. No, you will be asked to get involved in every area of your spiritual children's lives.

You will teach them the things that you do not learn in a book. Many times I have taken my spiritual children shopping to pick out clothes to change an image. As these things come into line, I can take them a step further.

I am there to teach them how to stand up and preach with confidence. I instruct them on how to minister personally, present a public prophetic word or master a strumming technique on the guitar.

I can imagine Jesus doing the same with his disciples around the campfire. He shared so many intimate things with them.

Sometimes you just need the honest input from someone standing on the outside. There are very few people in the world who are willing to pay that price. It is not easy to confront and to chisel, but as a spiritual parent you will be called upon to do both!

You will be called upon to shape the lives of those under you and you will need to teach and help them in every area. This will mean that you need to learn about these areas first.

So let the learning begin and realize that you never come to a place where you will stop learning and growing. As long as there are others receiving from you, you will need to continue changing yourself.

4. The Process of Re-parenting

I would have to say from personal experience that the toughest part of being a spiritual parent is taking each one through the process of re-parenting. All of us have been forged by our experiences in life. If you understand much concerning templates, you will know that much of this shaping was done by our natural parents.

Most parents did not know the principles I have taught so far. They failed or perhaps did not know the Lord at all. And so the foundation that your spiritual child's life is based on has quite a few cracks in it.

The only way to overcome it, would be to re-parent them and to fix the mistakes that were made by their natural parents. This can be tough, because it means dealing with all the bitterness and negative experiences in that person.

Often they will pour out all that anger on you! You will find yourself facing a spiritual child that is throwing a tantrum. Instead of walking away, as a spiritual parent it is your responsibility to follow through, to address and to heal those wounds of the past.

Then it is also for you to show them the correct way to respond. By being an example and also by getting involved in that person's life, the Holy Spirit will use you to reshape them into a vessel of glory.

This is no easy task, which explains why spiritual parenting is not found so readily in the Church. It is also why Apostle Paul says, "You have many instructors, but not many fathers." It is a hefty price to pay to follow through with a person like this.

It is a price one called to the Apostolic is required to pay.

5. Bearing the Burden

The greatest price a spiritual father pays is taking on the load of responsibility of his spiritual children. This is a spiritual load that you can only understand when you have taken that load for yourself.

It is not about the work or how much you have to do. It is a spiritual care that Paul speaks about often in the New Testament. Often we hear him say, *"2 Corinthians 11:28 besides the other things, what comes upon me daily: my deep concern for all the churches."*

The care that he speaks of, is something that will weigh heavily on you as a spiritual father. Taking responsibility for other people's lives is a heavy load because when you make a mistake, the buck stops at you.

You have to take the responsibility for that mistake, knowing that you have caused someone else to suffer because of your error. This in itself is a very heavy load to bear and it can be really discouraging at times.

Yet when you come to realize that the Lord takes responsibility for you also, you will come to a place of rest. There will be times when you make mistakes and there will be times when you fail, but the key is to keep getting up and allowing the Lord to cover you.

No matter what you have done, if you did it with the right intentions and in the name of the Lord, He will cover you. The price you pay will be in private when you fall on your face before the Lord, just like Moses did time and time again.

And so as we are nearing the end of our journey, I pray that you have begun to see the full picture of what the Lord has called you to. You need to decide now if you are willing to pay the price that is required of you and all that you will go through.

Count the cost as the scriptures say and then head out towards the horizon with hope in your heart and the goal in sight, knowing that the Holy Spirit will be the wind in your sails and the sun on the horizon!

Apostolic Authority

Chapter 18 – Apostolic Authority

Most of the time I am a terrible pushover with my kids. I try to put on the "tough face" but they know better. They know that if they ask Mom for anything, that I am likely going to say yes.

I guess it is the liberty we have as mothers. We are allowed to bend the rules a little. Unfortunately, though those rules get bent just too far and I am confronted with nothing short of chaos.

That is until Dad comes along to bring the balance. There are times when they cross the line just too far and Dad steps in with a single word.

A single word is all it takes and they are right in line. It comes with authority and from the first syllable they know, "Do *not* mess with him!"

Isn't it something, that from a young age already children can identify this authority? You do not need to teach the concept to them. When someone stands in real authority, they submit. It is a natural mechanism that the Lord has put into us.

Look at everyone you know and you will see those that have authority and those that just pretend. This is even more true in the spiritual realm.

You have so many folks running around these days calling themselves apostles, but how do you pick out those with a real call? One of the most obvious signs are the ones with true apostolic authority.

They are the ones that from the first syllable stop you dead in your tracks. You hear their voice and you cannot help but say, "Do *not* mess with him! That is the voice of God speaking!"

Spotting the Apostle

So how do you spot the apostle in the crowd? He is the one that carries an authority that is different to everyone else. When he speaks, you cannot help but know that what he says will come to pass.

I came to experience this as I trained the prophets in our first prophetic school. We used to give each student an evaluation that they would return for us to assess. Then as I read it over and sought the Lord on their behalf I would respond with where I saw them along their journey and what God had for their future.

As I wrote I would find an authority rise up and I would find myself saying things like,

"You will be facing a nine month periods of intense training where many things will be stripped from you.

The Lord is going to remove some relationships and put you on a new path. He is going to take you to a secret place for a season and you will find all your ministry opportunities beginning to close. Yet do not be discouraged, because at the end of this season, He will raise you up again and you will be released into the calling He has for you."

Where did that come from? At first I felt a bit apprehensive because it was so direct and I was not used to speaking prophetically in this way. At that time, as I sent these students what God gave me, I would hear from them about nine months down the road and they would say, "Do you remember what you said to me in my evaluation? Every single thing you said would happen ...did!"

There is Power in Those Words!

So what made the difference here? Was it my ability to hear God correctly? Was it my faith? Rather it was the authority of God that caused those things to come to pass. As I made myself available, His authority rose up from within me and as I spoke, I spoke into existence His plan for that person. It had nothing to do with my ability and everything to do with His authority!

Without that authority, you are an empty vessel. You might look like an apostle on the outside. You might even convince people that you are an apostle, but until you have that power in your words, you do not carry the authority of the apostle. So how do you identify an apostle? You identify them by the authority of Christ in their words and actions!

In an age where everyone wants to sit around and talk about everything that they have accomplished and what their plans are, the apostle who stands up and speaks with authority and brings change to the lives of God's people is the apostle that God will use to lay the foundation for the End Times Church!

Your Mandate is in Your Mouth!

So often you will find yourself running around, trying to make things happen in the natural that you forget a very powerful principle: Your mandate is in your mouth! I share in *Prophetic Essentials* how the power of God is released into the earth through words and actions.

So if you are going to bring God's plan about in your life and ministry it is going to begin with speaking forth creative words of authority into the earth.

But we like to be in control, don't we? We like to say, "I built up this ministry from nothing" and "I gave up everything I had in time, money and effort to make this ministry what it is today." But are you willing to put aside all of your doing for a bit and spend it speaking out those words of decree that will make it happen?

You are forgetting one very important principle here, it is not you who called you, but God who called you and as Paul says, *Philippians 2:13 For it is God who works in you both to will and to do for His good pleasure.*

It is God working in you that will bring about the mandate that He has given you. But yet the temptation is still there to jump in and make it happen. When the Lord first gives you a picture of what you want to do, you want to dive head first into the project and make it work! I cannot tell you how many bumps I have on my head from diving into the deep waters before the Lord told me to jump!

At times I could imagine the Lord standing there beginning a conversation with me, to tell me what He has planned and then right in the middle of Him talking to me, I begin running around in one hundred different directions, frantically trying to make it work. I can almost imagine Him finding a comfy spot to sit as He watched me, shaking His head, as I wore myself out.

Then again I could imagine Him giving me a knowing smile as I came back, having failed and exhausted, falling at His feet saying, "What happened? What did I do wrong?" Then He would need to take me to the first step again and paint the full picture for me, because I missed half of it in my zeal! Does that sound a bit like you? If so, do not be discouraged it is part and parcel of the many pitfalls you will face in apostolic preparation and training!

Getting the Full Picture

To begin speaking with authority, you first need to get the full picture. You need to know who you are in the Lord and you need to know what your mandate is. Until you can see clearly what He has called you to do, how could you have authority?

By Colette Toach

You see, Craig has the authority in our home. When he corrects the kids, he has every right to do so and to feel confident doing so.

He does not have that same confidence to walk into someone else's home to try and tell their kids what to do, because it is not his place.

It is the same for you. Until you know what you have authority over and know who and what you are, how could you possibly speak with that authority?

How can you stand and speak as an apostle, when you are not sure if you are in apostolic office yet? Until you know what you are and God has shown you where you are at, you will not have the confidence to use the authority that He has allocated to you.

My primary mandate has always been to train up the fivefold ministry. And so when a prophetic, apostolic or any of our other students needed to be corrected or responded to, I did it with confidence knowing that this is where God had placed me and that this was the task He has given me to accomplish.

I came to learn that when I spoke under the inspiration of the Holy Spirit into the life of another person, that what I spoke would come to pass. I was no longer just giving words of direction or words of knowledge, but I was speaking forth decrees that caused God's plan to come to pass!

Is this not what Moses did when he said, *Acts 3:22 For Moses truly said to the fathers, The Lord your God will raise up for you a Prophet like me from your brethren. Him you shall hear in all things, whatever He says to you."* And so he decreed the coming of Jesus! He was not tickling their ears; he was speaking under the inspiration of the Holy Spirit that caused that very thing to come to pass.

So before you can even begin speaking into the lives of people, start with knowing what your calling is and what garden the Lord has put you in. Because when you know that, then you have a place to start and you can begin looking to the Lord for that authority!

How Does It Come?

I am sure that if there is one question you have for me right now it is this, "So how do I get this authority then?" Is it something that you have to work for, fast for or pray for? Well how did Jesus get His authority?

> *John 17:1 Jesus spoke these words, lifted up His eyes to heaven, and said: "Father, the hour has come. Glorify Your Son, that Your Son also may glorify You,*
>
> *2 As You have given Him authority over all flesh, that He should give eternal life to as many as You have given Him."*

Jesus got His authority from the Father! And then something incredible happened...

"Matthew 28:18 And Jesus came and spoke to them, saying, "All authority has been given to Me in heaven and on earth.

19 Go therefore and make disciples of all the nations, baptizing them in the name of the Father and of the Son and of the Holy Spirit,"

...He gave that authority to us! That authority is found in Jesus. It is found in knowing Him and being conformed to His image. This is nothing that you can buy with money. It is nothing that you can study for and it is nothing that you can qualify for. For the qualification that is required for this authority is perfect and I am afraid that all of us fall short of that. No, the only way that you are going to gain that kind of authority is through Jesus and the work that He has done.

This really does mess with the concept of jumping in and doing everything alone, doesn't it? Could it possibly be that this authority does not come from your abilities or worth, but rather from your submission to the gentle hand of Jesus?

Oh how many people are willing to die for this authority, but how few know the all they need to do is *love* for this authority! For it is in loving the Lord Jesus and sacrificing your life unto Him that you will find this authority come into your life.

I remember the first time I began identifying that the words I spoke, were just not idle words any more. The

Lord Jesus had drawn me into the secret place and daily I spent time hiding away with Him there. There was a phase where I saw Him take me by the hand and lead me to a mountain. I saw a waterfall falling off the side of this mountain and as He took my hand He led me behind the waterfall to reveal a cave in the rocks.

I remember standing in that place in the spirit, with the sound of thundering in my ears and the wet mist of the water on my face as the Lord beckoned me to sit. It was just him and me and there was nothing else in that room besides us, the water and rocks.

He told me that He had drawn me there for a season where I must learn from Him and put aside all my visions, goals and desires for a season. It was a very special time in my life and it was here that He began stirring up the teaching ministry He had given me.

I did not know how much time passed as we spent time together day by day. Maybe it was a month or two. But I was so busy learning and drinking in the things that He would share with me every day that I did not even notice that I had changed. The time came when He led me out of that place and back into active ministry. It was then I noticed that things were just not the same. My words were not the same, I did not see things the same way and when I stood to minister, things happened! People were convicted and the Word of God came to life right before my eyes.

By Colette Toach

The Need for Recognition

So what price did I pay for this authority? Did I have to deprive myself or try to live a holy life? No, I just had to spend some time alone with Jesus. You know, you get so busy working *for* Him sometimes that you forget to just be *with* Him. It is in His tender presence that you are going to find the authority that you are seeking.

How many people strive all of their lives for their fathers to notice them? How many are trying to get others just to recognize their worth? And in the world we live in, unless you are the fittest, most intelligent or gifted, you do not make the grade. In many homes, unless you are the best child, your father does not show you how proud he is of you. And so you try hard to gain that recognition from him.

The strangest thing is that your father can even die and you will still find yourself doing and striving. You come to do the work of the Lord and still you strive. You stay up until early hours taking care of the flock. You work through holidays to make sure the ministry is cared for and you even forgo time with your family for the sake of the work.

Is it really the work of God that is driving you, or is it your need to find that recognition you so desire?

I have some news for you. Our heavenly Father accepted you from the day of your birth and whether you stay at home and do nothing or work hard all day, He will use you the same and make the same gifts and authority available to you! This parable is such a good example of that:

> *Matthew 20:1 "For the kingdom of heaven is like a landowner who went out early in the morning to hire laborers for his vineyard.*
>
> *2 Now when he had agreed with the laborers for a denarius a day, he sent them into his vineyard.*
>
> *3 And he went out about the third hour and saw others standing idle in the marketplace,*
>
> *4 and said to them, 'You also go into the vineyard, and whatever is right I will give you. 'So they went.*
>
> *5 Again he went out about the sixth and the ninth hour, and did likewise. 6 And about the eleventh hour he went out and found others standing idle, and said to them, 'Why have you been standing here idle all day?'*
>
> *7 They said to him, 'Because no one hired us. 'He said to them, 'You also go into the vineyard, and whatever is right you will receive.'*
>
> *8 "So when evening had come, the owner of the vineyard said to his steward, 'Call the laborers and give them their wages, beginning with the last to the first.'*
>
> *9 And when those came who were hired about the eleventh hour, they each received a denarius.*

10 But when the first came, they supposed that they would receive more; and they likewise received each a denarius.

11 And when they had received it, they complained against the landowner,

12 saying, 'These last men have worked only one hour, and you made them equal to us who have borne the burden and the heat of the day.'

13 But he answered one of them and said, 'Friend, I am doing you no wrong. Did you not agree with me for a denarius?

14 Take what is yours and go your way. I wish to give to this last man the same as to you.

15 Is it not lawful for me to do what I wish with my own things? Or is your eye evil because I am good?'

16 So the last will be first, and the first last. For many are called, but few chosen."

You see, it did not matter who worked the hardest and who worked the longest, it was only their obedience that counted and so all were given the same reward. Your Heavenly Father is just and He does not measure you by the same standards that your natural father measured you, or that you measure yourself by. He measures you through the perfect blood of Christ and do you know what happens when He does that? He sees you as perfect too!

All the "doing" in this world will not give you the reward you are looking for. Only Jesus can give you that authority and when you obey Him and hear His voice, you will find that reward begin manifesting in your life without you having to "work it up".

For many think that to be an apostle is to try and have authority, but they have it all wrong! Only when you have that authority are you an apostle and to find that authority you need to run away with Jesus.

Jesus is the source of everything that you need and everything that you are looking for. It is in Him that you will find the glory and the power that you seek to change the body of Christ. Realize that it has nothing to do with you. As I lived through this struggle myself, the Lord gave me a song and some of the words went like this:

> "The shaking, it will come.
> But, not because of you.
> Not because of what you do,
> But because of who I am
> Because of My glory
> Reflected in you."

The change you are looking for will come, but it will not come because of what you do, but because of who He is.

So take this opportunity to hide away with Jesus for a while. Take the phone of the hook, disconnect your internet connection, put a "do not disturb" sign on the door and do something that you probably have not done in a long time. Have a long heart to heart talk with Jesus.

Apostolic Ministry Step By Step

Chapter 19 – Apostolic Ministry Step by Step

What you need to know if you are called to be an apostle

As you have made this voyage with me from what an apostle looks like to where you fit into the big picture, perhaps you have identified the storms in your life. Perhaps you have embraced the land that awaits you.

Before you close this book and get on with your life, let me take your hand one final time and share some key principles with you that I have learned myself that will prepare you for the rest of the journey that lies ahead.

I cannot walk the rest of the way with you. You must learn these lessons yourself and you must grow under the covering of the hand of the Holy Spirit. I can point the road out to you. I can help charter your course, but at the end of the day, when you sail – you sail alone.

And so it is with any apostle called to take their place in the Church. What I can do is give you some directions to hide in your heart and to meditate on.

1. Without Jesus You do Not Exist

The scripture says that Jesus gave the apostles to the Church and without Him you do not exist. Sometimes it is so tempting to get caught up in "ministry" that you forget to minister to the person that is more important than anyone else.

If you run to His arms often and keep your eyes in His, you will walk over any mountain and through any river.

There have been so many times in my apostolic walk, when I looked at the road ahead of me and I would get weak thinking that I could not make it. I would cry out to the Lord and tell Him that this was just too difficult for me.

Each time He would smile lovingly and just say, "Look into my eyes. Do not look at the storms or your mountains. Just look into my eyes and when you do that you will look down to see that you have walked on water." Time and time again I have looked down to see the water beneath my feet, in awe of how much I managed to cope with.

Jesus will never withdraw His hand from you and when you get too busy or you forget to take that hand is when you will find your foot slipping. Run to Him! Hide in Him. He will be there when no one else is there.

He will love you when no one else cares and He will understand when no one else does. Only Jesus can know how it feels when you are going through inner struggles and only He can sooth that aching.

He understands your weaknesses and your failures and loves you in spite of them. So run to Him and hold Him close every day of your walk and you will move mountains without even having to try.

2. You Work for God, Not Man

When you are concerned about the responsibilities you have and the many people that need ministry, keep this point in mind. You work for God and not man.

Stop for a moment and ask God what you must do first and what should follow after that. It seems so simple, but sometimes you can get so caught up in your mistakes or in the many people that need a healing touch, that you think you have to do everything in your own strength.

So never forget that God is your boss. He pays your bills and He takes care of your needs. Follow the direction that He gives you and not after your obligations or after those things that you think you should be doing.

Very often the Lord may have a different task for you than you anticipated. So keep your ear close to His heart and wake up every morning asking Him what to do for that day. If you obey His voice and do those things that He tells you to do then nothing that man can do will hinder you.

Who cares what man thinks anyway? God is your boss and if they do not like it, then they can take it up with Him!

3. It is Okay to be Weak

In a society when only the fittest make it, it is no wonder that you try so hard to be a head above the rest. But I want you to know that it really is ok to be weak. Do not be afraid to show your heart to your spouse and your family.

The Lord has given them to you so that they might hold you up. The Lord never expected you to handle this load all on your own. He gave Miriam and Aaron to Moses and He gave David His mighty men. So do not try to be a lone warrior.

Share your heart with your spouse, children and family the Lord has given you. Share your fears and your weaknesses. Let them see your heart and as you open up like that, the Lord will move on them to meet your needs.

When you are in a ministry when you need to be strong for everyone else, it will set you free to know that it is alright to be weak at home. It does not make you less of a leader to admit that you need help. In fact, it makes you that much more of a leader because you are willing to be open and transparent.

4. You Have Nothing to Prove

When you discover that you have an apostolic calling, you get this feeling like you need to start doing something so that others will believe that you are called. When the time does come for you to stand in full apostolic authority, then you will not care about what others think because you will just stand in what you are.

You will not need to prove anything. If you are struggling with the fact that others cannot tell that you are an apostle, just keep walking the road of apostolic training and forget about trying to prove anything.

It reminds me of when my youngest daughter Ruby was still a baby. Every time someone saw her, they would say what a cute little boy she was. You see she was just too young for anyone to tell what gender she was.

It took a few years for people to easily see that she was a little girl. Well the same is with your calling. You know you have an apostolic call, but it is going to take a few years of maturing and growing up before it is evident to others.

By trying to tell others what you are and what God has called you to do, will not help you in any way. Just keep walking that road and soon enough they will notice that authority without you having to say anything. The Lord indeed is your vindicator. So leave Him to vindicate and prove His calling on your life and you just walk that calling out with fear and trembling!

5. Remain Humble and Teachable

When I have apostles come to me for training that give me a long list of their accomplishments and how they already know so much I often have to break the news to them that until they are willing to admit that they know nothing – they are nowhere near ready for training!

If you cannot adopt this attitude early in your apostolic training, then you are in for a very bumpy ride. Be as a sponge during the time of your training and receive everything that the Holy Spirit gives you.

Many of those times He will use others to teach you and it will be humbling for you to submit and receive from those that perhaps you think are beneath you. Yet if you are willing to admit that you are ignorant and that you have a long way to go, then the Lord has much more to work with. If you are already broken, then He can build upon you and if you are already empty then He can fill you.

However, if your mind is already filled with ideas and teachings, He will need to empty it first. And if you are already confident that you know everything, then He will have to strip your confidence away in your knowledge before He can begin.

So be like a child and just be prepared to admit that you are nowhere near ready for apostolic training.

It reminds me of the instruction that Jesus gave the Pharisees at one of their banquets. Seeing how all of them were trying to sit in a place of prominence, He told them to rather take a less prominent seat. In this way the head of the home could tell them to move forward and take a better seat.

Jesus shared how this was better than having to face the embarrassment of being told by the head of the home to take a lesser seat because you had taken a seat too far above your position!

The same applies to the apostolic calling. Rather be prepared to admit that you are immature and young in your calling and have the Holy Spirit surprise you with a sudden promotion, than be adamant that you have arrived and do not have much to learn, only to face the crushing realization that you are only at the starting line.

6. Judge No Man

It is really difficult not to get angry with those who are not prepared to move on with the things of God. There are many leaders in the Church that choose to remain stagnant and to dig their heels in and even oppose the New Move of God. It is so tempting to accuse them in return and to use everything in your means to prove your mandate.

Paul is very clear on you judging no man. He says that the Lord will bring the hidden things to light and reveal the intents of the heart of man. It is not for you to reveal the intents by using your own flesh. You need to realize that the revelation that God has given you, He has not given to them and this is why they cannot understand or see what God is doing in your life.

God has given them a different path to yours and whether they are being faithful to walk the path that He has given them or not does not depend on you. Simply walk the road God has given you to walk and leave them to walk theirs.

7. Wait to be Appointed

You are not an apostle until you are appointed by the laying on of hands. When was it that David became king as he was promised? It was when that crown was placed upon his head and he took his place upon the throne.

And so even though you might have a conviction of your calling and even received many prophetic words, until you have been officially placed in office by the agency of the Holy Spirit by the laying on of hands, you are not an apostle.

If even Jesus had to be released by John the Baptist, then surely you are no exception! You will find that your time of appointment will come when you least expect it and it will come through the agency of another prophet or apostle.

This is not something that you can do yourself. You can follow through the tests and the trials but until another lays their hands upon you and appoints you to this office, you cannot know that you fully stand in it.

You cannot wake up one morning and suddenly be in apostolic office. You cannot, after a little bit of training and hard trials say to yourself, "I have gone through all of what was described here, that means I must be in apostolic office!"

It does not work that way. You should be able to recall a specific time when you were appointed to apostolic office and you will know such a time well because along with it will come the apostolic authority that we have spoken about before. This authority is miraculous and you can call yourself what you will, until you stand in that authority you are not an apostle.

This is something that I have had open debate on with many when I challenged their position. I would have a student apply for our apostolic training saying that they are apostles. As I assess their calling I do not sense that apostolic authority.

It has nothing to do with your accomplishment or even what you have been through. That anointing and authority is given by God alone through the laying on of hands. Until you have experienced the release by the laying on of hands and that new authority and anointing on you, then press on until the time comes.

As the crown is placed on your head and you are seated upon the throne, you will know without a doubt what you are called to and you will wield that authority correctly.

Apostolic Office Step By Step

Chapter 20 – Apostolic Office Step by Step

The Truth About What Happens When You are in Apostolic Office

As you have embraced the preparation and training have you stopped to think what will happen when you finally are placed in apostolic office?

You have paid so many prices and gone through so much, but do you know what awaits you?

What will it look like on "the other side?" What will it feel like to finally be an apostle and to have been placed in that office? Well it is very different to what you expect and so I want to leave you with a short list of points that I pray you receive in your heart.

Make a note of them because you will live them. You will come to experience them and then you will pass them on to others who think that the call to apostleship is one of glory...

1. Your Apostleship is all About Giving It Up!

Now that might sound strange to you. However, the more you do the work of the Lord as an apostle you will come to learn that the more foundations you lay and the more patterns you put together, the more God will ask you to lay your apostleship aside.

You must never rest on your calling and on your title, but on the finished work of Calvary. I cannot tell you the number of times the Lord asked me to give that up.

Many times He has asked me to minister and never share who He has made me or what my calling is. He has said time and time again that the anointing on my life must stand for itself. When you can come to lay aside what you have worked so many years to attain, then Jesus can truly shine through you.

2. If You Aren't an Apostle in Your Weakness, You Aren't an Apostle at All

What a difficult lesson this was for me to learn. It is easy to be an apostle when you are standing behind the pulpit. It is easy to be an apostle when you are standing in front of a crowd and calling out revelations.

It is not easy to feel like an apostle when you have been woken up a number of times by a child that is having bad dreams or to minister to someone in need when you are having a bad day.

It is not easy to be an apostle when the Lord suddenly puts you in a place where you are not comfortable. It is not easy if you have a problem relating socially to people or are unable to open your heart to others.

It is hard to feel like an apostle when everyone else is laughing and joking and you feel like the outsider.

When you can come to realize that you are an apostle not because of what you *do* but because of what you *are*, your life will never be the same. Apostleship is not a once a week job, it is something you are all of the time.

You are an apostle when you wake up in the morning. You are an apostle when you get dressed. You are an apostle when you go to the bathroom. You are an apostle every moment of the day. That means that you should be living as one. All of the time!

If you have to try and be an apostle or try to maintain a standard, then you have a few more things to learn and perhaps unlearn before you can reach maturity.

3. The Learning Never Stops

Haven't you ever noticed how when you start studying a subject that the first thing you learn is how ignorant you are? Well the more you begin walking in your calling, the more you will come to realize how little you know and how little you have done.

As an apostle you will always be learning and changing. Whether the Lord suddenly calls you to learn a new skill or to take on a new kind of ministry, you are always learning and changing. Get used to it, because if you think it is bad when you are in preparation or training, you have not seen what it is like when you are actually in apostolic office.

4. The Fire is Your Best Friend

If you think that you experienced death during prep and training – you have not tasted anything yet. From the day you walk into apostolic office, the heat of the refining fire turns up. You will come to understand what Paul spoke about when he said, "I die daily."

Why is this? Well for every time that God needs to use you to meet a need in His people, He has to make sure you are able to do it!

It is very normal for Craig and me to go through an intense time of death and dealings before any conference or seminar. Each seminar is different and the people there have different needs.

So the Lord will put us through intensive training just for that conference. We will live the lessons we need to teach and we will overcome the problems that those attending will have. Then when we stand to speak, we speak from experience and by revelation, having lived through and overcome the same things that they are living right now.

5. You are Shaped and Reshaped.

This point follows on nicely from the last one. Just when you think you are to function in one capacity the Lord will change it according to the need of the people. This is why you face so much in prep and training.

From temperamental to cultural and social changes you will learn to minister to any person anywhere. You are like a piece of clay that will be taken and broken and reused many times by the Master.

That is what your calling is: to be all things when they are needed. If the Lord needs an evangelist for an evening, then you will be an evangelist. If he needs you to be a pastor for a season, then that is what you will be.

When people get to know you, they will not know what you are! For some groups will come to know you as a prophet and others as a teacher. You will never get the privileges of wearing a specific title. When this begins to happen to you then rejoice because you are just being an apostle.

6. I am an Apostle. I Can do Anything!

Craig and I always laugh at this statement. We came up with it when the Lord was leading all of us in so many new directions. It would seem that the Lord would just not allow us to take the easy way out in anything!

We just never had the luxury of getting others to help us and even though we complained more than once, I have come to see how it caused us to grow in every aspect of our lives.

As an apostle if there is a job to do, you should be able to do it. If you do not know how to do that job – then you learn. It is that simple.

By just walking this call out, you will find yourself accomplishing things that you never thought were possible! From leading praise and worship, playing various instruments, writing books, making books, cutting music CD's producing DVD's and so many other skills.

It has enabled us to reach more people and teach in a way that is alive and comes from personal experience.

7. The Pains of Labor do Pass.

Nothing can really prepare you for what is ahead other than experience and walking it out. This voyage is very much like giving birth and going through many contractions. But there is a good ending to this story.

After the travail is over and you look down at the baby that you have brought forth, you do not think about the pain any more.

At the time that you are facing the pressures you wonder why you started this journey and you feel like you want to give in. But there is nothing that even comes close to standing in His power and glory.

When you stand up to minister and find yourself saying things that are not from your own mind and see the lives of those you minister to turned around, you forget every death you ever faced.

So be encouraged, because the most exciting part about standing in the fullness of apostolic office is seeing the seeds that God planted in your heart produce fruit in the hearts of those you minister to.

8. Rejection is No Longer an Issue

When you are going through preparation and training it seems that every rejection hits you harder than you would care to admit. When you come to the place of knowing who you are in the Lord and stand in His authority rejection no longer becomes an issue in your life. You no longer face that rejection and you no longer care either.

You come to know that it is not about how good you are, but in just BEING. I seem to be saying that over and over again, but in my repetition I am praying that you will get that revelation for yourself.

Your voyage is not about accomplishing and building ministries and about doing, it is about being and being forged into a vessel fit for the Master's use.

9. You Begin to Appreciate Your Own Father.

When you have children of your own, you suddenly appreciate all the things that your own parents did for you. Well the spiritual walk is the same. As you rise up into apostolic office, you begin to appreciate all those who reared you when you were so arrogant and rebellious.

We would all like to think that we were the perfect spiritual child, but just wait until the Lord gives you a spiritual child that is just like you!

10. You Get Used to Being Different.

When you first start out it is really difficult being the odd one out all the time. For a large part of your preparation you spend your time just trying to fit in. When you finally get the point that you are meant to be different, you try to accept it but still struggle with the fact.

When you come to that place of knowing and being, you come to realize that you are the normal one here and that everyone else is different! It is not arrogance, but a security in who you are, and in what the Lord made you.

11. You are Confident Enough to Abase.

After striving and trying to be the best leader that you can be, you finally come to the place where you are just happy to be the deacon if that is what God wants. Even though the apostolic office is the highest, when you finally get there it really does not mean anything to you.

You minister when God wants you to minister. You do what God wants you to do.

I was joking with my family and saying to them, "You know I have a new saying lately. It goes like this

"...Whatever Lord!" Whatever He wants me to do; wherever He wants me to go. I do not care if He puts me in front of a huge crowd to preach or tells me to stay at home and spend some time helping my kids clean their bedroom.

When you come to standing in the apostolic office and receive the fullness of the image that God has given you, you do not need to try and be the highest ministry office.

For you come to learn that your calling does not lie in your doing or in your abilities or in your talents, but in the grace of God. God called you. God raised you up and God places you in that office. It is then His choice as to where He wants to put you and what He wants to do with you. When you come to that place of rest, you will think back on these words and you will understand. Apostolic maturity is indeed a place of rest.

12. Your Journey Has Just Begun.

The most startling realization when you finally reach apostolic office is that you have gone through all this preparation and this training only to discover that you qualified for your real journey to begin!

All the rest was just a preview of what the Lord wants you to do. It is humbling to look back on your life and all the trials you faced to know that they were all just little tests and trials to prepare you for a greater thing.

When you finally die to all those little accomplishments the Lord finally releases you into your real mandate. So if you are in training right now and you think you know what your mandate is. Give it a few years, because it will all change.

What you think you know and what you think you will do are nothing compared to the place the Lord will take you when you finally get to your destination. If He had to tell you ahead of time, both you and the enemy would mess it up. So expect to be surprised because the mandate that the Lord finally gives you when you come to the burning bush is nothing like you expected it to be!

Apostle in training the road is open before you and the Lord is going to lead you in many new and exciting directions. Perhaps after reading this book you have a picture in your mind of what to expect. Keep the book on hand, because as you live it, you will come back to it time and time again and see your life in its pages.

Parting Vision. Take up Your Baton

A few years ago the Lord gave me a vision that has stayed with me all this time. He showed me how through time He has raised up many men and women to carry His baton in prayer. He said to me that through time that He had raised up many who were hidden to intercede and to pray for the things that we are seeing right now.

He said how He had given them a baton to carry in their lives and then as they passed on how that baton was given to the next generation to carry it forward.

Then He said to me, "Now it is your turn to carry the baton that has been passed through generations. Only you will get to see what they did not see and you will eat the fruits of the prayers that they prayed. For the very decrees that they spoke in secret and the many hours that they travailed, you will see being manifest in my church."

That is such a powerful thought and as I take the baton that the Lord Jesus gave me to carry, I pass it on to you now. May you take it and carry it to the nations. May you rise up and take your place in the Church. May the Holy Spirit come upon you and shape you and cause you to be molded to His image.

May you take the hand of the Bride and marry her to her Groom and may you lay a new foundation for the Church. May you usher in the New Move and above all may you adorn and beautify the Bride for Jesus so that when He looks upon her He sees her in all of her glory! Amen.

Recommendations by the Author

If you enjoyed this book, we know you will also love the following books on the apostolic.

How to Get People to Follow You

By Colette Toach

"You have the potential for something magnificent, but until you can get your boat into the water and unfurl those sails... you are not going anywhere. " - Colette Toach

Colette pours out leadership secrets straight from the Throne Room that will make you the kind of leader others want to follow. No more hitting your head on the wall. No more being the only one excited about your vision.

Sharing from her own failures and triumphs, Colette hands you the keys to your success as a leader.

You Will Learn:

1. **The one thing that will get others to automatically admire you**
2. **The two things that keep making people run from your leadership**
3. **How to get others excited about your vision**
4. **How to get the kind of loyalty that will get others to follow you to the ends of the earth**

5. **The 3 phases of God's leadership training - Where are you?**
6. **How to identify your open doors**
7. **How to win the heart of the public**
8. **How to win the hearts of those on your team**

Just like Gideon, David, Peter and Moses who weren't born leaders, but were forged into leaders - so you can have the kind of crowd that will follow you anywhere. There is a strong leader inside of you yet. One who is admired, loved and sought out! Learn how to get people to follow you and fulfill the vision that God has given you.

Called to the Ministry

By Colette Toach

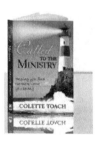

God has put a purpose for your existence inside you. There is a driving force within you to accomplish something much greater than yourself and to fulfill the call of God on your life.

However, how do you know what that calling is?

Apostle Colette Toach takes you by the hand and helps you to realize the call of God that has been whispering to you all along.

By Colette Toach

It is the conviction of your calling that will fuel the fire to push through when times get rough. By teaching you how to KNOW His will for you and to hear clearly from Him, you will receive the conviction that will push you through the fire time and time again.

Learn how to experience His presence and you will no longer need not feel lost or insecure about the choices you will make. When you know how to get a rhema word from God, nothing can stop you from moving forward.

Then as you realize your calling, map out the training that is sure to come. Each fivefold ministry training is geared to shape you into a certain kind of vessel. Apostle Colette goes the extra mile and explains in detail which one(s) you will go through and what it is going to produce in you.

By the end of this book, you will know too much. So much so that you will be held accountable for fulfilling your call. There will be no more excuses as to why you cannot succeed. Apostle Colette releases an anointing in this book that will challenge, convict, motivate and launch you into your calling!

Fivefold Ministry School

When God called me to the ministry the term "Fivefold Ministry" was hardly seen in the church. So for the Lord to say that I was called to be a prophet... then a teacher... then an apostle... blew my mind!

Where Do you go to Train for the Fivefold?

At first I did not get it. One minute the Lord told me I was a prophet. The next He informed me that I was in teacher training. Then just as I got nice and comfortable with the balance that the teacher brings, God had me step out as an evangelist. Imagine my confusion for a minute when after all that, He told me to "Pastor His flock."

My head was spinning! "God which of the Fivefold have you called me to?"

His reply: *"I have called you to live all of the fivefold ministry - so that you can train others!"*

Suddenly the words of Apostle Paul made sense. When he told the churches that they would eat the fruit of his labor I understood my calling. This training, the years I spent in the desert and even more years pouring into others so they could rise up ahead of me... all made sense.

By Colette Toach

My calling? To help you fulfill yours! So not matter which of the Fivefold Ministry you are called to, together with my team, we can equip you in it!

Having passed through each of these trainings and lived through the crucible of experience, I am ready to give you what you need to succeed.

You Can be a Success in Ministry!

My passion is to see you realize yours! I understand the years in the desert. I know what it feels like to have a fire shut up in your bones, knowing that God has something greater for you.

That is why together with my husband Craig Toach, we have trained up our own Fivefold Ministry team and in association with apostles all over the world, we hold in our hands the resources to launch you into your ministry!

Not only do we provide specialized fivefold ministry training, we also provide fivefold ministry assessment, personal mentorship, interactive fellowship with other students and once you qualify - certification, credentials and promotion of your ministry.

http://www.fivefold-school.com/

Contacting Us

Go to www.ami-bookshop.com to check out our wide selection of materials.

Do you have any questions about any products?

Contact us at: +1 (760) 466 - 7679
(8am to 5pm California Time, Weekdays Only)

E-mail Address: admin@ami-bookshop.com

Postal Address:

> A.M.I
> 5663 Balboa Ave #416
> San Diego, CA 92111, USA

Facebook page:
http://www.facebook.com/ApostolicMovementInternational

YouTube page:
https://www.youtube.com/c/ApostolicMovementInternational

Twitter Page: https://twitter.com/apmoveint

AMI Bookshop – It's not Just Knowledge, It's **Living Knowledge**

Made in the USA
Middletown, DE
26 February 2018